Oswald and Ruby in Dallas
Where They Lived, Loved
Worked and Murdered
A Self-Guided Tour

―――――――

Michael Reid

Oswald and Ruby in Dallas. Where They Lived, Loved, Worked and Murdered. A Self-Guided Tour. Copyright © 2015 by High Street Press

For Joe and Jack

Table of Contents

Introduction 6

Key Events 8

Lee Harvey Oswald

Timeline - Lee Harvey Oswald 9

Jaggers-Chiles-Stovall/525 Browder 22

Oswald stayed here/604 Elsbeth 24

Oswald lived here/214 W Neely St 26

Downtown Dallas Post Office/400 N Ervay 29

Edwin Walker house/4011 Turtle Creek Blvd 32

Oswald stayed here/621 N Marsalis 37

Santa Fe Building/1114 Commerce 39

Oswald stayed here/1026 N Beckley 40

Morning News/the motorcade route 41

Ruth Paine Museum/2515 W Fifth Irving 43

Texas School Book Depository/411 Elm 47

Sixth Floor Museum/411 Elm 52

Dealey Plaza 55

Oswald's movements after the shooting 60

Greyhound Bus Station/205 Lamar St 68

Tippit murder site/East 10th St and Patton 70

The Texas Theater/211 W Jefferson 75

Dallas Municipal Building/106 S Harwood 82

Parkland Hospital/5201 Harry Hines Blvd 90

Shannon Rose Hill Memorial Park   95

The Ozzie Rabbit Lounge   97

The JFK Memorial/646 Main St   98

Jack Ruby

Timeline – Jack Ruby   99

Ruby lived here/1917 ½ Ervay   104

Ruby lived here/3929 Rawlins   105

Ruby lived here/500 N Marsalis   106

Bob Wills Ranch House   107

Alice Nichols, Ruby's girlfriend   108

The Carousel Club/1312 ½ Commerce   110

The Adolphus Hotel/1321 Commerce   115

Lucas B&B Restaurant/3520 Oak Lawn   116

Campisi's Egyptian/5610 E Mockingbird   117

The Oak Cliff neighborhood   120

Cliff Sanitary Grocery   121

Dobb's House restaurant   123

Ruby's apartment/223 S Ewing   124

The Tour   131

Introduction

Walt Cisco, Dallas Morning News - JFK-Motorcadee.gif, Penn Jones Photographs. Baylor University Collections of Political Materials. Waco, Texas.

This guide is for those who want to see Oswald and Ruby sites in Dallas, but do not want to go on a guided tour or spend the time to organize a tour themselves. All the important places are here and even some the tours do not include. The guide provides directions for getting from place to place via the shortest routes and in an organized fashion so you do not waste time. You can use the directions or plug the addresses into your GPS. It takes less than a day to visit all the places, depending on how much time you spend at each one.

The book also includes Warren Commission witness testimony related to many of the sites. The Warren Commission was established by President Johnson to investigate the assassination of JFK. The Commission's final report came out in September 1964 and two months later twenty-six volumes of supporting documents were published. The supporting documents include the testimony of 552 witnesses.

Some have maligned The Warren Commission. We make no claims as to the accuracy or inaccuracy of Warren Commission conclusions. And included here are not Commission conclusions, but raw excerpts from interviews with eyewitnesses, people who were actually at these sites when the events occurred. With these first-hand accounts, you may be able to get a better sense of what happened and come to your own conclusions.

Key Events

Here is a review of key events in the assassination of President John Fitzgerald Kennedy.

1. November 21, 1963. Lee Harvey Oswald goes to the house in Irving, Texas where his wife and two small children are staying. He secretly retrieves his rifle hidden in a rug in the garage.

2. November 22, 1963. Oswald goes to work at the Texas Book Depository, hiding the rifle in a long paper bag. He builds a sniper's nest on the 6th floor of the depository and fires three shots, two of which hit President Kennedy. The President is later pronounced dead at Parkland Hospital.

3. After the shooting, Oswald flees from the Depository. He takes a taxi to his rooming house in the Oak Cliff neighborhood, gets his handgun and leaves on foot. Shortly thereafter, he kills Dallas Police Officer J.D. Tippit.

4. Oswald is apprehended at the Texas Theater and taken to Dallas Police Headquarters where he is charged with Tippit's murder and the murder of President Kennedy.

5. November 24, 1963. Nightclub owner Jack Ruby shoots Oswald.   Oswald is pronounced dead at Parkland Hospital.

Timeline – Lee Harvey Oswald

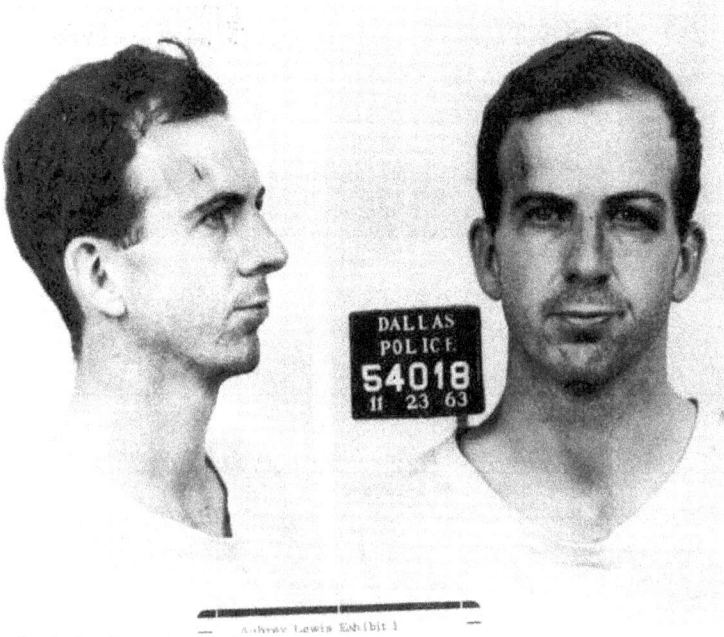

Dallas Police Department photo

Lee Harvey Oswald was 24 years old when he died on an operating table in Parkland Hospital in Dallas. In his adult life, he lived in Dallas only about nine months. He spent more time in New Orleans (where he was born), Fort Worth (where he went to school), New York City (where he was truant most of the time), Japan (in the Marines) and the Soviet Union (as a defector) than he did in Dallas.

Oswald always seemed to be dissatisfied. He badly wanted to get into the Marines, but once a soldier, he wanted out. He wanted to live in the Soviet Union, but spent half his time there trying to leave. He married a Soviet citizen and brought her to the United States, but tried to get her to go back to Russia. In the United States after returning from the Soviet Union, he wanted to defect to Cuba. He needed to work, but once he had a job he slacked off and was repeatedly fired for poor work or for not working at all.

Oswald was quite capable of violence. He beat his wife regularly and with such severity that neighbors feared for her life. Before murdering President Kennedy, he attempted to assassinate a far-right political figure.

He never made much above minimum wage and left an estate of about $200 in cash and a cheap wedding band. In addition, he left a wife who could barely speak English and two small children, the youngest one month old.

Oswald's Mother – New Orleans

- July 20, 1933: Lee's mother (Marguerite) marries Robert Oswald (father of LHO). This is her second marriage.

- August 19, 1939: Robert Oswald, Sr. dies before Lee is born.

New Orleans. October 1939 – January 1944 (about 4 1/4 years)
- October 18,1939. Oswald is born in New Orleans, Louisiana.

Dallas. January 1944 – Fall 1945 (not quite 2 years)
- January 1944. Oswald and his mother move to Dallas.

- May 1945: Marguerite marries Edwin A. Ekdahl.

Ft. Worth. Fall 1945 – August 1952 (almost 7 years)
- Fall 1945. Marguerite and Lee move to Benbrook, a suburb of Ft. Worth.

- October 1945. Lee starts at Benbrook Commons School.

- February 1946. Lee is admitted to Harris Hospital in Fort Worth for acute mastoiditis. He undergoes an operation to remove part of the mastoid bone behind the ear to drain infection.

- January 1947. Marguerite and Lee move into Fort Worth proper.

- May 1947. Lee completes the 1st grade at Clayton Elementary. The next school year, he starts 2nd grade at Clayton.

- Summer, 1947: Marguerite discovers Ekdahl is having an affair and confronts him.

- January 1948. Marguerite orders Ekdahl out. She and Lee move to 3300 Willing Street in Fort Worth.

- March 1948. Lee starts at George C. Clark Elementary mid-March 1948. He graduates from the 2nd grade.

- June 1948. Marguerite's divorce from her Ekdahl is final.

- Fall 1948. Marguerite buys a 2-bedroom home at 7408 Ewing. Lee attends Arlington Heights Elementary.

- September 1949. Lee transfers to Ridgelea West Elementary. He attends Ridgelea for 3 years.

The Bronx, New York City. August 1952 – January 1954 (1 ½ years)
- August 1952. Marguerite sells the Ewing Street house and she and Lee move to New York City to live with Lee's brother John.

- August 1952. Lee attends Trinity Evangelical Lutheran School for several weeks and then transfers to Public School 117, a junior high school in the Bronx. He is 13 years old.

- Lee and Marguerite move to 1455 Sheridan Avenue in the Bronx just off the Bronx Grand Concourse.

- 1952. Lee beings to skip school. During one period, he is absent 47 out of 62 days. He spends much of his time either at home alone or at the Bronx Zoo.

- January 1952. Marguerite and Lee move to 825 E 179th street in the Bronx. Lee transfers to PS 44. January 15, 1952 – March 11, 1953, he does not attend any classes.

- April 1953. Due to his truancy, Lee is remanded to Youth House (a detention home for delinquent boys) for 3 weeks of psychiatric study.

- May 10, 1953. Oswald obtains a handout about Julius and Ethel Rosenberg. This begins his interest in Marxism.

New Orleans. January 1954 – July 1956 (almost 2 ½ years)
- January 1954. Marguerite and Lee leave New York and go to New Orleans where they stay with Marguerite's sister. Lee attends Beauregard Junior High. His attendance improves.

- Early 1954. They move to an apartment on St. Mary Street.

- April 1955. They move to 126 Exchange Place in April 1955

- Lee joins the Civil Air Patrol with another boy from school. He drops out after 2 – 3 meetings.

- Fall 1955. He enters 10th grade at Warren Easton High School.

- October 1955. Lee presents a falsified letter to Easton saying he is moving to San Diego. When the school calls, Marguerite covers for him. She also falsifies a letter to the Marine Corps saying he is age 16.

- November 1955. Lee gets a job as a messenger boy -- $130/month (about 75 cents an hour). He quits the job after a couple of months.

- January 1956. Oswald gets a job as office boy and runner. This job lasts two weeks. Shortly thereafter, he is hired as messenger for a dental lab.

Fort Worth. July 1956 – October 1956 (about 4 months)

- July 1956. Oswald and his mother move to Fort Worth. Lee is 16 years old. This is the 17th time he and his mother have moved.

- September 1956. Lee enrolls at Arlington Heights High School, but drops out before the end of the month.

- October 3, 1956: Oswald contacts the Socialist Party of America.

Lee Harvey Oswald - Marine

mypetjawa.mu.nu

The United States Marine Corps. October 1956 – September 1959 (almost 3 years)

- October 1956. Oswald enlists in the Marines on his 17th birthday.

- He takes a bus to Dallas for a physical and then flies to San Diego. Oswald arrives in San Diego October 26, 1956. At age 17, Oswald is 5'8" and 135 pounds. In the Marines, he makes $78/month. When he is discharged in September 1959 as Private 1st Class, Oswald is making $108/month (about $834 in 2015 dollars).

- December 21, 1956: Oswald scores 212 (Sharpshooter) on a marksmanship test.

- Oswald undergoes 10 weeks of basic training in San Diego, and is then transferred in January 1957 to the Infantry Training Regiment, Camp Pendleton.

- May 1, 1957. Oswald is promoted to Private 1st Class.

- August 22, 1957. Oswald embarks on the USS Bexar to Yokosuka, Japan for duty at Atsugi Naval Air Station.

- October 1957. Oswald shoots himself with his own gun.

- June 1958. Oswald is court-martialed for having a personal weapon and for verbally assaulting and pouring a drink on a non-commissioned officer. He spends 48 days confinement at hard labor and is thereafter assigned full-time to mess hall duty.

- September 16, 1958. Oswald is in sickbay with gonorrhea.

- November 1958. Leaves Atsugi and arrives in San Francisco. He takes leave in Ft. Worth.

- December 1958. Oswald is stationed at El Toro in California. In March 1959 he is promoted back to Private 1st Class.

- August 1959. He receives an early discharge based on hardship - his mother had injured her nose.

- September 4, 1959. Oswald applies for passport.

- September 11, 1959. Oswald is released from active duty. A year later he receives a "dishonorable discharge."

The Soviet Union. October 1959 – 1962 (2 ½ yrs)
- Arrives in Fort Worth September 14, 1959 and leaves for New Orleans a few days later.

- September 20, 1959. Oswald leaves New Orleans on a ship for Le Havre, France.

- October 8, 1959. Docks at Le Havre. He is 10 days shy of 20th birthday.

- October 9, 1959. He goes to London and flies on to Helsinki, Finland.

- October 15, 1959. Oswald enters the Soviet Union via train and arrives in Moscow on October 16, 1959.

Oswald in the Soviet Union (wearing the sunglasses)

www.russianbooks.org

- October 21, 1959. The Soviet Union rejects his application to defect and Oswald attempts suicide.

- October 31, 1959: Oswald goes to the American Embassy and tries to renounce his American Citizenship. Nothing is ever done by the embassy to terminate Oswald's U.S.A. citizenship.

- Jan 4, 1960. The Soviets reconsider and allow Oswald to stay in the country. Broke, he is given $500 by the Soviet Red Cross.

- January 7, 1960. Oswald travels to Minsk and works in a radio and television factory.

- September 1960. Oswald receives a "dishonorable discharge" from the Marines.

- February 1961. The American Embassy in Moscow receives a letter from Oswald saying that he wants to return to the U.S.A.

- April 30, 1961. He marries Marina Prusakova, a Soviet citizen.

- February 15, 1962. Oswald's daughter, June Lee, is born. Oswald is 21 years of age.

- May 23, 1962. Oswald, his wife and baby leave Minsk for Moscow.

- June 1, 1962. Oswald obtains a loan from the embassy for $435.71.

- June 4, 1962. The Oswald family sails for the United States from Rotterdam, Holland.

- Oswald was in Soviet Union for a little over 2 ½ years. For half of that time, he was trying to get out.

Fort Worth. June 1962 – October 1962 (almost 5 months)

- June 14, 1962. Oswald and family fly to Dallas and live with Lee's brother Robert in Fort Worth, then move in with his mother for about a month.

- June 26, 1962. The FBI interviews Oswald for the first time about his stay in the Soviet Union.

- July 1962. Oswald gets a sheet metal job that pays $1.25/hour (that is $50 a week working a 40-hour week; $386/week in 2015 dollars). The minimum wage in 1962 was $1.15/hour. Oswald rents an apartment at 2703 Mercedes Street in Fort Worth.

- August 16, 1962. The FBI interviews Oswald a second time.

- October 8, 1962. He walks out on his job.

Dallas. October 1962 – April 1963 (7 months)

- October 8 1962 - takes a bus to Dallas and gets a job at a graphic arts firm – Jaggers-Chiles-Stovall - at $1.35/hour.

- Oswald uses the company's photo equipment to forge a new identity, including a Selective Service card, in the name of Alek J. Hidell. He opens a Post Office Box to receive mail for Hidell and himself.

- October 15, 1962. Moves into the YMCA and stays through October 19.

- November 3, 1962 – Rents an apartment for $68 dollars/month at 604 Elsbeth Street in the Oak Cliff neighborhood of Dallas. On November 4th, his wife and baby move in.

- November 5, 1962. The Oswalds have an argument. Marina and the baby go to a friend's house to live. Marina and the baby return to 604 Elsbeth on November 17.

- January 27, 1963 - orders a handgun via mail order.

- March 1963. Fighting between Lee and Marina becomes intolerable for other tenants. The landlord tells them to stop fighting or leave. They move to 214 West Neely Street.

- March 1963. Oswald orders a Mannlicher-Carcano carbine via mail order.

- April 1, 1963. Oswald is fired from his job.

- April 10, 1963. Oswald fails in his attempt to assassinate General Edwin Walker. He fires at Walker from the alley behind Walker's house as Walker is working on his taxes. The bullet strikes a window frame and is deflected.

New Orleans. April 1963 – September 1963 (about 5 months)
- April 24, 1963. Oswald takes a bus to New Orleans and stays with his aunt Lillian.

- May 1963. He gets at a job at a coffee company as a general laborer and rents an apartment at 4907 Magazine Street. Marina and June arrive shortly thereafter.

- June 16, 1963. Oswald distributes pro-Cuba pamphlets at the Dumaine Street Wharf.

- June 24. Oswald applies for a new passport.

- July 19. Oswald is fired from his job for poor work. He lives on unemployment compensation until middle of August 1963.

- July 25, 1963. Oswald's request for a review of his "undesirable discharge" is denied.

- August 9, 1963. Oswald hands out pro-Cuba pamphlets on Canal Street. He is arrested for disturbing the peace and spends the night in jail.

Below: Oswald handing out "Fair Play for Cuba" leaflets

commons.wikimedia.org

- September 23, 1963. Marina and June leave for Dallas with Marina's friend Ruth Paine.

- September 25, 1963. Oswald collects his $33 unemployment check and leaves New Orleans for Mexico City.

Mexico City. September 27, 1963 – October 2, 1963 (6 days)

- September 27, 1963. Oswald arrives in Mexico City by bus. He goes to the Cuban and Soviet embassies seeking a visa for travel to Cuba.

- Both the Cubans and Soviets refuse to provide him with a visa.

- October 2, 1963. Oswald leaves Mexico City on a bus.

Dallas. October 2, 1963 - November 24, 1963 (54 days)

- October 3, 1963. Oswald arrives in Dallas and checks into the YMCA. He files a claim for unemployment compensation.

- October 4, 1963. He goes to Ruth Paine's house in Irving (a suburb of Dallas) where Marina is staying. Oswald spends the weekend there.

- October 7. Oswald rents a room at 621 North Marsalis in the Oak Cliff neighborhood of Dallas. The landlady kicks him out after a week.

- October 14, 1963. Oswald rents a room at 1026 North Beckley Avenue. He registers as O.H. Lee.

- October 16, 1963. Oswald starts work at Texas School Book Depository.

- October 20, 1963. Marina gives birth to a baby girl – Audrey Marina Rachel Oswald - at Parkland Hospital.

- November 1963. On two occasions, FBI Agent James Hosty travels to Irving to talk to Oswald. Oswald is not there and instead Hosty interviews Ruth Paine and her neighbors. In 1975, Mr. Hosty admitted receiving a note from Oswald in the weeks prior to the assassination. He said he destroyed it on November 24, 1963 on orders from his supervisor, the day Jack Ruby shot Oswald. According to Hosty, Oswald complained in the letter about Hosty questioning his wife Marina.

- Oswald lives at 1026 North Beckley during the week and visits Marina and the two children on the weekends in Irving.

- November 19, 1963. *The Dallas Morning News* publishes the presidential motorcade route.

- November 21, 1963. Oswald gets a ride to Ruth Paine's house in Irving. While there, he secretly retrieves his rifle hidden in a rug in the garage.

- November 22, 1963. Oswald goes to work at the Texas School Book Depository. He brings the rifle into the Depository in a paper bag and builds a sniper's nest on the 6th floor. Oswald fires three shots, two of which hit President Kennedy.

- After the shooting, Oswald flees from the Depository, leaving his rifle. He takes a taxi to his rooming house, gets his handgun and leaves on foot. Shortly thereafter, he kills Dallas Police Officer J.D. Tippit. Oswald is apprehended at the Texas Theater.

- November 24, 1963. Jack Ruby shoots Oswald. Oswald is later pronounced dead at Parkland Hospital.

Forth Worth
- Oswald is buried at Shannon Rose Hill Memorial Park, Fort Worth, TX.

Jaggers-Chiles-Stovall
525 Browder
(the building is no longer there)

www.metaltype.co.uk

In October 1962, Oswald got a job at Jaggers-Chiles-Stovall in Dallas at $1.35 an hour. At the end of March 1963, he was fired for sub-standard work (with a 10-day notice making his last day April 6, 1963).

In testimony to the Warren Commission, the President of JCS said that after Oswald was fired, another company called and asked for a reference on Oswald. The executive checked and found out "This fellow was kind of an oddball, and he was kinda peculiar sometimes and that he had had some knowledge of the Russian language, which--this is all I knew, so I told Ted [from the company wanting the reference], I said, 'Ted, I don't know, this guy may be a damn Communist... If I was you, I wouldn't hire him.'"

22

In additional testimony, the President of JCS said, "There was such a short period of time this fellow worked for us and he was a constant source of irritation because of his lack of productive ability... We would ask him to reduce a line to 4 inches in width, that happened to be 6, and he might make it 4 1/4 or 3 7/8, and this was a loss in labor and materials both, and it had to be redone."

Oswald lived here – 604 Elsbeth

On November 3, 1962, Oswald rented a $68/month apartment (about $525 in 2015 dollars) at 604 Elsbeth in the Oak Cliff neighborhood of Dallas (this was shortly after he got the job at Jaggers-Chiles-Stovall). The Oswald family moved in the next day. They lived at the address until March 1963 when they were asked to leave because of noise complaints from other tenants.

The 10-unit complex was built in 1925. By 2008, the building was in bad repair and deemed a safety hazard. The City of Dallas sued to have it demolished and it was torn down at the end of 2012.

One-time Oswald house to be demolished. November 30, 2012. Houston Chronicle.

Mr. and Mrs. Tobias, the managers of the apartments at 604 Elsbeth, gave the following testimony to the Warren Commission. The testimony was given to Mr. Albert E. Jenner, Jr., assistant counsel of the Commission.

Mr. TOBIAS. Well, I talked to her [Marina, Oswald's wife] and, of course, she wouldn't say nothing back and Oswald, I tried to talk to him several times and all I could get out of him was a grunt. He was a kind of a guy that wouldn't talk to you at all.

Mr. JENNER. Is that right?

Mr. TOBIAS. Yes; and he was a peculiar duck.

Mr. JENNER. How did your other tenants feel toward Oswald?

Mr. TOBIAS. Well, they didn't like it.

Mr. JENNER. They didn't like what?

Mr. TOBIAS. They didn't like the way he beat her all the time.

Mr. JENNER. They complained to you that he manhandled her?

Mr. TOBIAS. Yes; there was one man that came over there one night and he told me, he said, "I think that man over there is going to kill that girl," and I said, "I can't do a darn thing about it." I says, "That's domestic troubles."

Below: The owner of 604 Elsbeth in Oswald's old apartment

One-time Oswald house to be demolished. November 30, 2012. Houston Chronicle.

Oswald lived here
214 West Neely Street

From 604 Elsbeth, the Oswalds moved to 214 Neely (March 3, 1963), transporting their belongings in a baby carriage. Just nine days later, on March 12, 1963 Oswald ordered a carbine via mail order. It was in the backyard of this house that Marina photographed Oswald with his rifle, a handgun and Marxist literature. Oswald was living here when he attempted to assassinate Edwin Walker on April 10, 1963.

www.citylab.com

This is a private home. The people who live here typically charge several dollars to enter the backyard and take pictures.

26

Below: Oswald with his guns and Marxist literature. Photograph taken in the back yard at 214 West Neely Street.

Creative Commons/Google images

Testimony of the house's owner to the Warren Commission...

"M. Waldo George, 6769 Inverness Street, Dallas, being duly sworn says:

1. ...I am the owner of the premises at 214 Neely Street, Dallas, Texas, consisting of two apartments, one upper and one lower. In the latter part of January 1963 the upper apartment became vacant and I posted it "For Rent" by means of an appropriate sign in the yard in front of the premises.

27

2. On March 2, 1963, I was advised by Mrs. George that an individual by the name of "Oswald" had inquired about renting the apartment. Later that day I met the individual who identified himself as Lee H. Oswald. I advised him that the rent for the apartment was $60 per month, and he rented the apartment on a month-to-month basis, paying me $60 in cash for one month's rent in advance.

3. On April 1, 1963, I collected $60 in cash from Oswald, covering rent for the month of April 1963 to and including May 2, 1963.

4. Shortly after this occasion the downstairs tenants, Mr. and Mrs. George B. Gray, called me and informed me that the man in the upstairs apartment was beating his wife. I made no inquiry into this subject matter.

5. Two or three days later, myself and Mrs. George called on the Oswalds in their apartment and invited them to attend Gaston Avenue Baptist Church with us. He informed me and Mrs. George that he attended the Russian Orthodox Church although they were not regular in their attendance, because they had to depend on their friends to take them.

6. During this visit Oswald stated that he had met his wife while he was serving in the United States Marines as a guard at the United States Embassy in Russia, and had married his wife in Russia. I made direct inquiry of him as to whether he had had any difficulty in getting out of Russia with his wife and he said that he had had no difficulty whatsoever.

7. Neither myself or Mrs. George saw Oswald again at any time thereafter. Oswald did not pay rent for the succeeding rental period of May 2 through June 2, 1963. Because my attention was diverted by other matters, I did not go by the apartment to collect the rent for that period until several days after May 2, 1963. When I arrived at the apartment I found it vacant.

Downtown Dallas Post Office
400 N Ervay St

On October 9, 1962, Lee Harvey Oswald rented a box at the downtown Post Office. On March 12, 1963, Oswald (under his false identity Alek Hidell) ordered a rifle with scope via mail order from Klein's Sporting Goods in Chicago. He paid $19.95 plus shipping and handling and picked up the rifle at the Post Office on March 20.

www.unvisiteddallas.com

Testimony of William Waldman, Vice President at Klein's Sporting Goods, before the Warren Commission. Testimony given to Mr. David W. Belin, assistant counsel to the Commission.

Mr. BELIN... Now, I'm going to hand you what has been marked as Waldman Deposition Exhibit No. 7 and ask you to state if you know what this is.

Mr. WALDMAN. This is a copy made from our microfilm reader-printer of Dallas, Tex. I want to clarify that this is not the order, itself, received from Mr. Hidell, but it's a form created by us internally from an order received from Mr. Hidell on a small coupon taken from an advertisement of ours in a magazine.

Mr. BELIN. This Waldman Deposition Exhibit No. 7 is a print from the micro- film negative which we just viewed upstairs; is that correct?

Mr. WALDMAN. That's correct.

Mr. BELIN. And Waldman Deposition Exhibit No. 8 is also a print from the microfilm record we viewed upstairs showing the actual coupon and the envelope in which the coupon was enclosed; is that correct?

Mr. WALDMAN. That's correct.

Mr. BELIN. And do you have any general advertising program whereby you advertise in gun magazines?

Mr. WALDMAN. We do.

Mr. BELIN. Can you just give us one or more of the magazines in which this coupon might have been taken?

Mr. WALDMAN. Well, this coupon was specifically taken from American Rifleman Magazine, issue of February 1963. It's identified by the department number which is shown as--now, if I can read this--shown as Department 358 on the coupon.

Mr. BELIN. And that number also appears in the address on the envelope to you, is that correct, or to your company?

Mr. WALDMAN. That's correct.

Mr. BELIN. Now, I believe that you said the total amount was $19.95, plus $1.50 for shipping charges, or $21.45; is that correct?

Mr. WALDMAN. The $1.50 is for both shipping charges and handling.

Mr. BELIN. I hand you what has been marked as Commission Exhibit No. 788, which appears to be a U.S. postal money order payable to the order of Klein's Sporting Goods, and marked that it's from a purchaser named A. Hidell, and as the purchaser's street address is Post Office Box No. 2915, and the purchaser's City, Dallas, Tex.; March 12, 1963: and underneath the amount of $21.45, the number 2,202,130,462. And on the reverse side there appears to be an endorsement of a bank. I wonder if you would read that endorsement, if you would, and examine it, please.

Mr. WALDMAN. This is a stamped endorsement reading "Pay to the order of the First National Bank of Chicago," followed by our account No. 50 space 91144, and that, in turn, followed by "Klein's Sporting Goods, Inc."

Edwin Walker house
4011 Turtle Creek Boulevard

Oswald attempted to assassinate Major General Edwin Walker, (Retired) on April 10, 1963. Firing from the alley behind Walker's house, Oswald missed.

Edwin Walker was an American army officer who fought in World War II and Korea. Walker resigned his commission in 1961 after being reprimanded by the Joint Chiefs for calling Eleanor Roosevelt and Harry Truman "pink" and for trying to direct the votes of his troops. Walker had far-right views and was involved in attacks against Adlai Stevenson in Dallas and in distribution of anti-Kennedy leaflets on the day of the assassination. The leaflets read: "Wanted for Treason: JFK."

4011 Turtle Creek Boulevard

www.realtor.com

This is a private home and no tours are available.

General Edwin Walker

"Edwin A. Walker" by Unknown military photographer - U.S. War Department. Licensed under Public Domain via Wikimedia Commons

Testimony of Edwin Walker before the Warren Commission...

Mr. LIEBELER. It is my understanding that on the evening of April 10, 1963, some person fired a shot at you while you were in your home on Turtle Creek Boulevard; is that correct?

General WALKER. That is correct.

Mr. LIEBELER. Would you tell us the circumstances surrounding that event, as you can now recall them?

General WALKER. I was sitting behind my desk. It was right at 9 o'clock, and most of the lights were on in the house and the shades were up. I was sitting down behind a desk facing out from a corner, with my head over a pencil and paper working on my income tax when I heard a blast and a crack right over my head.

Mr. LIEBELER. What did you do then?

General WALKER. I thought--we had been fooling with the screens on the house and I thought that possibly somebody had thrown a firecracker, that it exploded right over my head through the window right behind me. Since there is a church back there, often there are children playing back there. Then I looked around and saw that the screen was not out, but was in the window, and this couldn't possibly happen, so I got up and walked around the desk and looked back where I was sitting and I saw a hole in the wall which would have been to my left while I was sitting to my right as I looked back, and the desk was catercornered in the corner up against this wall. I noticed there was a hole in the wall, so I went upstairs and got a pistol and came back down and went out the back door, taking a look to see what might have happened.

Warren Commission...

Note left by Oswald.---On December 2, 1963, Mrs. Ruth Paine turned over to the police some of the Oswalds' belongings, including a Russian volume entitled "Book of Useful Advice." In this book was an undated note written in Russian. In translation, the note read as follows:

1. This is the key to the mailbox which is located in the main post office in the city on Ervay Street. This is the same street where the drugstore, in which you always waited, is located. You will find the mailbox in the post office which is located 4 blocks from the drugstore on that street. I paid for the box last month so don't worry about it.

2. Send the information as to what has happened to me to the Embassy and include newspaper clippings (should there be anything about me in the newspapers). I believe that the Embassy will come quickly to your assistance on learning everything.

3. I paid the house rent on the 2d so don't worry about it.

4. Recently I also paid for water and gas.

5. The money from work will possibly be coming. The money will be sent to our post office box. Go to the bank and cash the check.

6. You can either throw out or give my clothing, etc. away. Do not keep these. However, I prefer that you hold on to my personal papers (military, civil, etc.).

7. Certain of my documents are in the small blue valise.

8. The address book can be found on my table in the study should need same.

9. We have friends here. The Red Cross also will help you [Red Cross in English].

10. I left you as much money as I could, $60 on the second of the month. You and the baby [apparently] can live for another 2 months using $10 per week.

11. If I am alive and taken prisoner, the city jail is located at the end of the bridge through which we always passed on going to the city (right in the beginning of the city after crossing the bridge).

Warren Commission...
According to Marina Oswald's testimony, on the night of the Walker shooting, her husband left their apartment on Neely Street shortly after dinner. She thought he was attending a class or was on his own business." When he failed to return by 10 or 10:30 p.m., Marina Oswald went to his room and discovered the note. She testified: "When he came back I asked him what had happened. He was very pale. I don't remember the exact time, but it was very late. And he told me not to ask him any questions. He only told me he had shot at General Walker." Oswald told his wife that he did not know whether he had hit Walker; according to Marina Oswald when he learned on the radio and in the newspapers the next day that he had missed, he said that he "was very sorry that he had not hit him." Marina Oswald's testimony was fully supported by the note itself which appeared to be the work of a man expecting to be killed, or imprisoned, or to disappear.

Oswald stayed here
621 North Marsalis

Returning from Mexico City, Oswald rented a room at 621 North Marsalis in Oak Cliff. The landlady disliked Oswald and kicked him out after a week. This is what she said in testimony to the Warren Commission, "I didn't like his attitude. He was just kind of like this, you know, just big shot, you know, and I didn't have anything to say to him, and-- but, I didn't like him. There was just something about him I didn't like or want him-- just wasn't the kind of person I wanted. Just didn't want him around me."

This address is now a vacant lot, but many of the homes on the block date from Oswald's time, so you can get a sense of what the neighborhood was then.

www.dallasnews.com

This same landlady saw Oswald right after the assassination boarding a city bus. "Oswald got on. He looks like a maniac. His sleeve was out here [indicating]. His shirt was undone... Was a hole in it, hole, and he was dirty, and I didn't look at him. I didn't want to know I even seen him, and I just looked off, and then about that time the motorman said the President had been shot..."

The Santa Fe Building
1114 Commerce Street/1118 Jackson Street

In 1963, the FBI field office was located in the Santa Fe Building. This is where Oswald delivered a note to Agent James Hosty telling him to quit harassing his wife and himself. Oswald delivered the note in the weeks leading up the assassination. Hosty later admitted that he destroyed the note on orders from his supervisor (apparently because he felt it would show the FBI had not been doing its job keeping track of Oswald).

"Sanatfe01" by Dfwcre8tive - Own work. Licensed under CC BY 3.0 via Wikimedia Commons

Oswald stayed here
1026 North Beckley Avenue

After Oswald was kicked out of 621 North Marsalis, he moved here on October 14, 1963. Seventeen other boarders were also living in the rooming house. Oswald's space was barely bigger than a closet. It was to this house that Oswald returned after shooting President Kennedy. He got his handgun and a jacket and left.

dallas.univision.com

The owners have kept Oswald's room the way it was in 1963. The same bed Oswald slept in is still there. Tours of the home are available for $20. See www.oswaldroominghousetours.com/

Mrs. Johnson, the owner of 1026 North Beckley at the time, gave the following testimony to the Warren Commission.
"Mr. BALL. Did you see him eat anything but lunch meat?

Mrs. JOHNSON. I never did, just lunch meat, all he ever put in there and preserves, I think he had some preserves and milk; but he put about a half gallon of sweet milk in that box each day.

......

Mr. BALL. Did he go out nights, any?

Mrs. JOHNSON. I just really never did see that man leave that room.

.....

Mr. BALL. He would watch television sometimes?

Mrs. JOHNSON. Yes, sir; watch television, with the other men renters and he wouldn't speak to them, Maybe they would speak to him but he wouldn't speak.

.....

Mr. BALL. Did he have any visitors?

Mrs. JOHNSON. No, sir; he never had a visitor."

Owner Pat Hall sits in Oswald's former room at 1026 N. Beckley.

"Two houses associated with Kennedy assassination added to National Register of Historic Places" Roy Appleton. dallasnews.com. December 12, 2014.

Dallas Morning News published the President's motorcade route on November 19, 1963

The newspaper published the motorcade route three days before President Kennedy's arrival. Unlike other presidential assassins, Oswald did not stalk his prey. President Kennedy came to him.

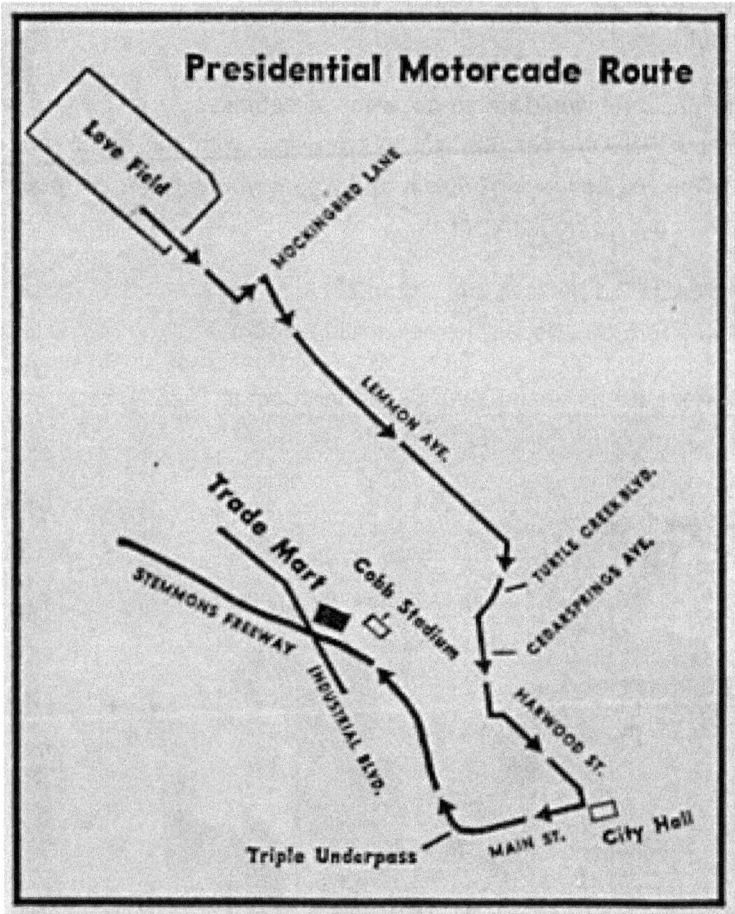

Dallas Morning News, front page. November 1963.

Ruth Paine House Museum
2515 West Fifth Street. Irving, Texas.

Oswald's wife Marina and their two small children were living in Irving, Texas at Ruth Paine's house when the assassination occurred. Ruth was a Russian speaker and a friend of Marina. Lee Oswald got a ride to the house the night before the assassination to pick up his rifle that was hidden in a rug in the garage.

In 2009, the City of Irving purchased the house and created a museum that is open to the public. The home's furnishings and décor have been restored to what they looked like in 1963.

cityofirving.com

You can drive to the house. It is in a residential neighborhood, but people in the area are used to seeing cars stopped in front of the dwelling.

If you want to go into the home, you have to sign up for a formal tour. The tour starts at the Irving Library and ends at The Ruth Paine house. Tours last 90 minutes and are limited to 12 people. Tour cost: Adult 12 and over - $12, Children 11 and younger – free. For information, call 972.721.3729.

The following are excerpts from Ruth Paine's testimony before the Warren Commission...

Mr. JENNER - Would you please give me your impression of Lee Oswald's personality, what you think made him tick, any foibles of his, your overall impression now as you have it sitting there of Lee Harvey Oswald?

Mrs. PAINE - My overall impression progressed through several stages.

Mr. JENNER - Why don't you give those. I think it would be helpful to us if you would. Start at the beginning.

Mrs. PAINE - In the spring what I knew of him was that he wanted to send his wife away back to the Soviet Union, which she didn't want to do, that he would not permit her to learn English or certainly didn't encourage it. I knew that he had lost his job and looked unsuccessfully. I formed an initial negative opinion about him, on really very little personal contact. I saw him very briefly the evening of the 22d of February, the evening of the second of April, and the afternoon of the 20th of April, and again on the 24th of April and so as far as I remember that is virtually all of the contact I had had directly with him. And this impression stayed with me throughout the summer and throughout my visits to various friends and family on my trip of August and September 1963, and I undoubtedly conveyed to the people I talked to during that time that impression, which I carried at that time. When I saw him again in New Orleans, beginning the 20th of September, I was impressed quite differently. He seemed friendly. He seemed grateful, as reported in this letter to my mother, even grateful that I was offering to have his wife in my home and help her make arrangements at Parkland Hospital to have the baby there, at a fee adjusted to their income. He appeared to me to be happy, called cheerily to Marina and June as he came in the house with a bag full of groceries. He, as I described, washed the dishes that evening that Marina and I went down to Bourbon Street. And particularly in parting on the morning of September 23 I felt he was really sorry to see them go. He kissed them both at the house as we first took off and then again when we left from the gas station where I had bought a tire. And I felt, as expressed in this letter that you just showed me to my mother that he hoped to have his family together again as soon as he could. Then, of course, the impression enlarged as I saw him in my home on the weekends beginning October 4, and I have read into the record one letter I wrote to my mother during that period, which shows that he tried to be helpful around the house, that he played with my children, that he, it appeared to me, was becoming more relaxed and less fearful of being rejected, and I had sensed in him this fear earlier. It was because I had sensed in him in the spring this insecurity and feelings of inadequacies that the thought once crossed my mind as expressed to Mrs. Rainy that he could be guilty of a crime of passion if he thought someone was taking away from him his wife, something valuable to him. Clearly he valued Marina. She was his only human contact, really, and I think while----

Mr. JENNER - His only human contact?

Mrs. PAINE - Really, so far as I could see, the only friend he had, and while he did quarrel and was petty with her on many times that I saw, he, I felt, valued her, and, of course, it is also true, as I have reported, that I never saw him physically violent to her or cruel, so that my impression of him, which I carried with me throughout my trip during the summer, changed, and my impression of him up to the time----

Mr. JENNER - Of the assassination?

45

Mrs. PAINE - Of the assassination, was of a struggling young man who wanted to support his family, who was having difficulty, who wanted to achieve something more in life than just the support of his family and raising children, who was very lonely, but yet could meet socially with people and be congenial when he made efforts to be.

.....

Mr. JENNER - Would you tell us of your feelings toward Marina? You liked her? That is what I am getting at.

Mrs. PAINE - Yes; I like her very much. I felt always that what I wanted to say and what I was able to understand of what she said was hampered by my poor Russian. It improved a good deal while with her, and we did have very personal talks about our respective marriages. But I felt this was just a developing friendship, not one in full bloom, by any means. I respected what I saw in her, her pride, her wish to be independent, her habit of hard work, and expecting to work, her devotion to her children, first to June and then to both of the little girls, and the concentration of her attention upon this job of mother, and of raising these children. I also respected her willingness and effort to get on with Lee, and to try to make the best of what apparently was not a particularly good marriage, but yet she had made that commitment and she expected to do her best for it.

Texas School Book Depository
411 Elm St

en.wikipedia.org

On November 22, 1963, Lee Harvey Oswald fired three shots from the sixth floor of the Texas School Book Depository. Two of those shots hit President Kenney. The building was purchased in 1977 by Dallas County and it is now known as the Dallas County Administration Building

The County renovated the first five floors for government offices. A bookstore on the first floor specializes in materials about Oswald and President Kennedy. The Sixth Floor Museum is located on the top two floors and includes the location where Oswald fired the shots. The sniper's nest has been recreated and you can see exactly where Oswald pulled the trigger.

Admission to the Sixth Floor Museum: Adult — $16.00, Senior (Ages 65+) — $14.00, Youth (Ages 6-18) — $13.00, Children (Ages 0-5) — Free or $4.00 U.S. with audio guide.

Testimony of Roy Truly, Oswald's supervisor at the Texas School Book Depository...

BELIN. All right. Now, what is your best estimate of the speed [of the Presidential limousine] as he started to go down the street here marked Parkway?

Mr. TRULY. He picked up a little speed along here, and then seemed to have fallen back into line, and I would say 10 or 12 miles an hour in this area.

Mr. BELIN. All right. Then what did you see happen?

Mr. TRULY. I heard an explosion, which I thought was a toy cannon or a loud firecracker from west of the building. Nothing happened at this first explosion. Everything was frozen. And immediately after two more explosions, which I realized that I thought was a gun, a rifle of some kind. The President's--I saw the President's car swerve to the left and stop somewheres down in this area. It is misleading here. And that is the last I saw of his car, because this crowd, when the third shot rang out--there was a large crowd all along this abutment here, this little wall, and there was some around us in front--they began screaming and falling to the ground. And the people in front of myself and Mr. Campbell surged back, either in terror or panic. They must have seen this thing. I became separated from Mr. Campbell. They just practically bore me back to the first step on the entrance of our building.

Mr. BELIN. When you saw the President's car seem to stop, how long did it appear to stop?

Mr. TRULY. It would be hard to say over a second or two or something like that. I didn't see I just saw it stop. I don't know. I didn't see it start up.

Mr. BELIN. Then you stopped looking at it, or you were distracted by something else?

Mr. TRULY. Yes. The crowd in front of me kind of congealed around me and bore me back through weight of numbers, and I lost sight of it. I think there were a lot of people trying to get out of the way of something. They didn't know what.

Mr. BELIN. Then what did you do or see?

Mr. TRULY. I heard a policeman in this area along here make a remark, "Oh, goddam," or something like that. I just remember that. It wasn't a motorcycle policeman. It was one of the Dallas policeman, I think-- words to that effect. I wouldn't know him. I just remember there was a policeman standing along in this area about 7, 8, or 10 feet from me. But as I came back here, and everybody was screaming and hollering, just moments later-I saw a young motorcycle policeman run up to the building, up the steps to the entrance of our building. He ran right by me. And he was pushing people out of the way. He pushed a number of people out of the way before he got to me. I saw him coming through, I believe. As he ran up the stairway--I mean up the steps, I was almost to the steps, I ran up and caught up with him. I believe I caught up with him inside the lobby of the building, or possibly the front steps. I don't remember that close. But I remember it occurred to me that this man wants on top of the building. He doesn't know the plan of the floor. And-that is- that just pepped in my mind, and I ran in with him. As we got in the lobby, almost on the inside of the first floor, this policeman asked me where the stairway is. And I said, "This way". And I ran diagonally across to the northwest corner of the building.

....

Mr. BELIN. This is to show this is a stairway, and there is a stairway above it, too. But you went up the stairs right here?

Mr. TRULY. That is right.

Mr. BELIN. Okay. And where was this officer at that time?

Mr. TRULY. This officer was right behind me and coming up the stairway. By the time I reached the second floor, the officer was a little further behind me than he was on the first floor, I assume--I know.

Mr. BELIN. Was he a few feet behind you then?

Mr. TRULY. He was a few feet. It is hard for me to tell. I ran right on around to my left, started to continue on up the stairway to the third floor, and on up.

...

Mr. BELIN: Now, as you raced around, how far did you start up the stairs towards the third floor there?

Mr. TRULY. I suppose I was up two or three steps before I realized the officer wasn't following me.

Mr. BELIN. Then what did you do?

Mr. TRULY. I came back to the second floor landing.

Mr. BELIN. What did you see?

Mr. TRULY. I heard some voices, or a voice, coming from the area of the lunchroom, or the inside vestibule...

Mr. BELIN. All right. And I see that there appears to be on the second floor diagram, a room marked lunchroom.

Mr. TRULY. That is right.

Mr. BELIN. What did you do then?

Mr. TRULY. I ran over and looked in this door... I saw the officer almost directly in the doorway of the lunch-room facing Lee Harvey Oswald.

Mr. BELIN. And where was Lee Harvey Oswald at the time you saw him?

Mr. TRULY. He was at the front of the lunchroom, not very far inside he was just inside the lunchroom door.

Mr. BELIN. ...What did you see or hear the officer say or do?

Mr. TRULY. When I reached there, the officer had his gun pointing at Oswald. The officer turned this way and said, "This man work here?" And I said, "Yes."

Mr. BELIN. And then what happened?

Mr. TRULY. Then we left Lee Harvey Oswald immediately and continued to run up the stairways until we reached the fifth floor.

Mr. BELIN. All right. Let me ask you this now. How far was the officer's gun from Lee Harvey Oswald when he asked the question?

Mr. TRULY. It would be hard for me to say, but it seemed to me like it was almost touching him.

....

Mr. BELIN. About how long did Officer Baker stand there with Lee Harvey Oswald after you saw them?

Mr. TRULY. He left him immediately after I told him--after he asked me, does this man work here. I said, yes. The officer left him immediately.

Mr. BELIN. Did you hear Lee Harvey Oswald say anything?

Mr. TRULY. Not a thing.

Mr. BELIN. Did you see any expression on his face? Or weren't you paying attention?

Mr. TRULY. He didn't seem to be excited or overly afraid or anything. He might have been a bit startled, like I might have been if somebody confronted me. But I cannot recall any change in expression of any kind on his face.

The Sixth Floor Museum in The Dallas County Administration Building
411 Elm St

Below: Displays in the Sixth Floor Museum

The sniper's nest at The Sixth Floor Museum

Sixth Floor Museum

Testimony of Luke Mooney, Deputy Sheriff of Dallas County, who searched the Texas School Book Depository immediately after the assassination...

Mr. MOONEY... I begin criss-crossing it, round and round, through boxes, looking at open windows---some of them were open over on the south side. And I believe they had started laying some flooring up there. I was checking the fire escapes. And criss-crossing back and forth. And then I decided--I saw there was another floor. And I said I would go up. So I went on up to the seventh floor. I approached Officers Webster and Vickery. They were up there in this little old stairway there that leads up into the attic. So we climbed up in there and looked around right quick. We didn't climb all the way into the attic, almost into it. We said this is too dark, we have got to have floodlights, because we can't see. And so somebody made a statement that they believed floodlights was on the way. And I later found out that probably Officers Boone and Walters had gone after lights. I heard that. And so we looked around up there for a short time. And then I says I am going back down on six. At that time, some news reporter, or press, I don't know who he was--he was calming up with a camera. Of course he wasn't taking any pictures. He was just looking, too, I assume. So I went back down ahead of Officers Vickery and Webster. They come in behind me down to the sixth floor. I went straight across to the southeast corner of the building, and I saw all these high boxes. Of course they were stacked all the way around over there. And I squeezed between two. And the minute I squeezed between these two stacks of boxes, I had to turn myself sideways to get in there that is when I saw the expended shells and the boxes that were stacked up looked to be a rest for the weapon. And, also, there was a slight crease in the top box. Whether the recoil made the crease or it was placed there before the shots were fired, I don't know. But, anyway, there was a very slight crease in the box, where the rifle could have lain--at the same angle that the shots were fired from. So, at that time, I didn't lay my hands on anything, because I wanted to save every evidence we could for fingerprints. So I leaned out the window, the same window from which the shots were fired, looked down, and I saw Sheriff Bill Decker and Captain Will Fritz standing right on the ground. Well, so I hollered, or signaled I hollered, I more or less hollered. I whistled a time or two before I got anybody to see me. And yet they was all looking that way, too except the sheriff, they wasn't looking up. And I told him to get the crime lab officers en route, that I had the location spotted. So I stood guard to see that no one disturbed anything until Captain Will Fritz approached with his group of officers, city officers.

Dealey Plaza – corner of Houston and Elm

www.richgscott.com

Dealey Plaza is where the assassination occurred. Both the Texas School Book Depository and the grassy knoll are here.

The Plaza is a park built in 1940 by the Works Progress Administration (the WPA was a depression-era agency that employed out-of-work Americans to build public works projects). It is located on the west edge of downtown Dallas where three streets converge – Main Street, Elm Street and Commerce Street.

The grassy knoll is on the northwest side of the plaza. It is just down the hill from the Texas School Book Depository. Further down the hill is a triple underpass beneath a railroad bridge, under which the Kennedy motorcade sped after the shooting.

Dealey Plaza is a National Historic Landmark and the buildings around it are, for the most part, those that were there in 1963. Many of the street lights and street signs in Dealey Plaza are also the same as in 1963.

Below: The grassy knoll.

dallas.about.com

There were 104 Dealey Plaza earwitnesses. 56 said the shots came from the direction of the Depository or the Houston and Elm Streets intersection. 35 witnesses said the shots came from the grassy knoll or the triple underpass. The remaining 13 witnesses mentioned other locations or said the shots came from multiple sources.

Testimony of Luke Mooney, Deputy Sheriff of Dallas County, who searched the Grassy Knoll upon hearing the shots...

Mr. BALL - Were you standing there when the President went by?

Mr. MOONEY - Yes, sir. I took my hat off.

Mr. BALL - That is on Main Street?

Mr. MOONEY - Right.

Mr. BALL - And that is--

Mr. MOONEY - 505 Main.

Mr. BALL - That is where the cavalcade turned north?

Mr. MOONEY - Made a right turn, yes, sir; on Houston Street.

Mr. BALL - That building is about a block south on Houston, isn't it--south of the Texas School Book Depository?

Mr. MOONEY - Yes, sir; it is a short block there.

Mr. BALL - After the President's car went by, what did you do?

Mr. MOONEY - Well, we were we was more or less milling around. We just kept standing there, more or less talking to one another. I don't know how many seconds had elapsed--it wasn't too many.

…..

Mr. BALL - What happened, as you remember?

Mr. MOONEY - After that few seconds elapsed, we heard this shot ring out. At that time, I didn't realize it was a shot. The wind was blowing pretty high, and, of course, it echoed. I turned my head this way.

Mr. BALL - You mean to the right?

Mr. MOONEY - To the right; yes, sir. We were facing more or less south. And I turned my head to the right.

Mr. BALL - That would be looking towards Houston Street?

Mr. MOONEY - Looking towards the old court. Well, when I turned my head to the right; yes, sir. I would be looking west. And there was a short lapse between these shots. I can still hear them very distinctly--between the first and second shot. The second and third shot was pretty close together, but there was a short lapse there between the first and second shot. Why, I don't know. But when that begin to take place after the first shot we started moving out. And by the time I started running--all of

57

us except Officer Ingrain he had a heart attack, and, of course, he wasn't qualified to do any running.

Mr. BALL - Which way?

Mr. MOONEY - Due west, across Houston Street, went down across this lawn, across Elm Street there--- I assume it is approximately the location the President was hit. Of course the motorcade was gone. There wasn't anything there except a bunch of people, a lot of them laying on the ground, taking on, various things. I was running at full speed.

Mr. BALL - When you ran across Elm, where did you go?

Mr. MOONEY - Across Elm, up the embankment, which is a high terrace there, across--there is a kind of concrete building there, more or less of a little park. Jumped over the fence and went into the railroad yards. And, of course, there was other officers over there. Who they were, I don't recall at this time. But Ralph Walters and I were running together. And we jumped into the railroad yards and began to look around there. And, of course, we didn't see anything there. Of course the other officers had checked into the car there, and didn't find anything, I don't believe, but a Negro porter. Of course there were quite a few spectators milling around behind us. We were trying to clear the area out and get all the civilians out that wasn't officers.

Mr. BALL - Why did you go over to the railroad yard?

Mr. MOONEY - Well, that was--from the echo of the shots, we thought they came from that direction.

Mr. BALL - That would be north and west from where you were standing?

Mr. MOONEY - Yes, sir. To a certain extent--northwest. The way the echo sounded, the cracking of the shot. And we wasn't there many second-- of course I never did look at my watch to see how many seconds it took us to run so many hundred yards there, and into the railroad yard. We were there only a few seconds until we had orders to cover the Texas Depository Building.

Oswald's movements after the shooting

Here is a recap of Oswald's movements after the shooting.

1. Three minutes after the shooting, Oswald exits the Texas School Book Depository and walks along Elm Street toward downtown for almost six blocks.

2. He boards a city bus (his former landlady sees him get on).

3. The bus takes Oswald back toward the scene of the shooting and becomes snarled in traffic.

4. Oswald exits the bus and goes on foot to the bus station.

5. He gets a cab at the bus station and goes to the Oak Cliff neighborhood. He has the cab drop him off several blocks away from his rooming house. NOTE: This may be the first time in Oswald's life that he has taken a cab. He always takes the bus, hitchhikes or gets a ride from someone.

6. Oswald walks to the rooming house, gets his handgun and a jacket and leaves.

7. He walks until stopped by Dallas Police Officer J.D. Tippit at 10th Street and Patton.

8. Oswald shoots Tippit. A dozen people witness the murder.

9. Oswald flees the scene, throwing away his jacket as he goes.

10. He attempts to hide in the Texas Theater.

11. After a scuffle during which Oswald tries to pull his gun, police arrest Oswald. The time is 1:50 PM. It is 1 hour 20 minutes since he shot President Kennedy.

The following three pages trace Oswald's movements after the shooting.   The first map is taken directly from the Warren Commission Report.   The subsequent maps are the same as in the Report, but redrawn to make them easier to read.

It is recommended that you walk the route in Insert A and then drive Insert B.

Warren Commission maps with Inserts A and B

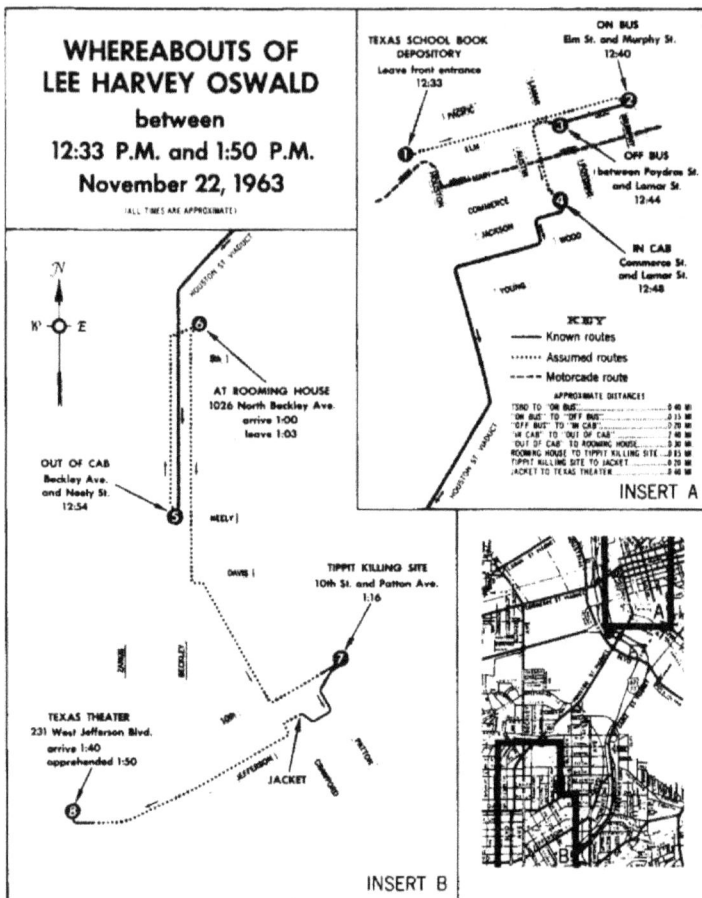

WHEREABOUTS OF LEE HARVEY OSWALD between 12:33 P.M. and 1:50 P.M. November 22, 1963

(ALL TIMES ARE APPROXIMATE)

TEXAS SCHOOL BOOK DEPOSITORY
Leave front entrance
12:33

ON BUS
Elm St. and Murphy St.
12:40

OFF BUS
(between Poydras St. and Lamar St.
12:44

IN CAB
Commerce St. and Lamar St.
12:48

KEY
— Known routes
······· Assumed routes
– – – Motorcade route

APPROXIMATE DISTANCES

INSERT A

AT ROOMING HOUSE
1026 North Beckley Ave.
arrive 1:00
leave 1:03

OUT OF CAB
Beckley Ave. and Neely St.
12:54

TIPPIT KILLING SITE
10th St. and Patton Ave.
1:16

TEXAS THEATER
231 West Jefferson Blvd.
arrive 1:40
apprehended 1:50

JACKET

INSERT B

COMMISSION EXHIBIT No. 1119-A

62

Insert A redrawn

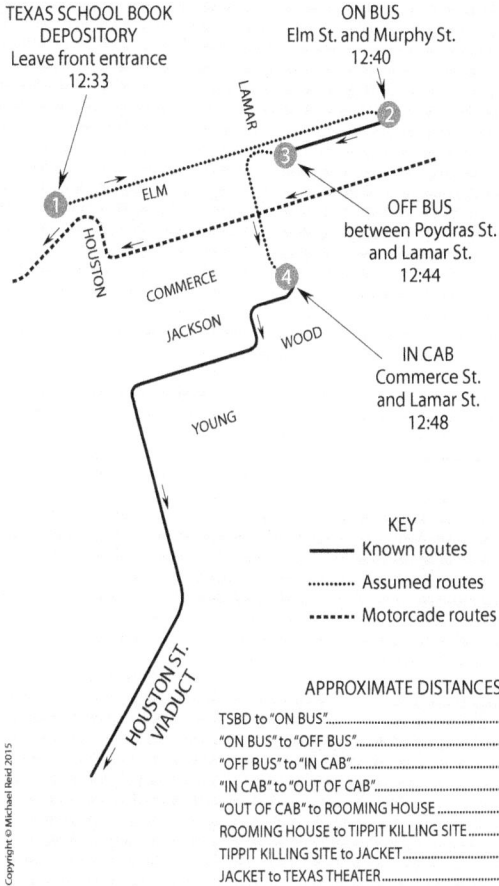

INSERT A

TEXAS SCHOOL BOOK DEPOSITORY
Leave front entrance
12:33

ON BUS
Elm St. and Murphy St.
12:40

LAMAR

ELM

HOUSTON

COMMERCE

JACKSON

WOOD

YOUNG

OFF BUS
between Poydras St.
and Lamar St.
12:44

IN CAB
Commerce St.
and Lamar St.
12:48

HOUSTON ST. VIADUCT

KEY
—— Known routes
·········· Assumed routes
------ Motorcade routes

APPROXIMATE DISTANCES

TSBD to "ON BUS"	0.40 mi.
"ON BUS" to "OFF BUS"	0.15 mi.
"OFF BUS" to "IN CAB"	0.20 mi.
"IN CAB" to "OUT OF CAB"	2.40 mi.
"OUT OF CAB" to ROOMING HOUSE	0.30 mi.
ROOMING HOUSE to TIPPIT KILLING SITE	0.15 mi.
TIPPIT KILLING SITE to JACKET	0.20 mi.
JACKET to TEXAS THEATER	0.40 mi.

Copyright © Michael Reid 2015

63

Insert A walking directions

1. Start at the Texas Book Depository (now called the Dallas County Administration Building).

2. Walk toward downtown Dallas on Elm Street. Go to the entrance to the Renaissance Tower office building located at 1234 Elm – 5 ½ blocks from the Depository. This is approximately where Oswald boarded the bus. NOTE: The Insert A map shows Oswald boarding the bus at Elm and Murphy Street. Murphy Street used to be between Griffin and Field, but no longer exists.

3. Now go back the way you came. This is the way the bus was moving (back toward the scene of the crime). Go to three-quarters of the way between Griffin and Lamar Streets - about 1 ¼ blocks. This is 911 Elm Street (Milliners Supply company is located there as of April 2015). Oswald got off the bus here when is got snarled in traffic. NOTE: The Insert A map says Oswald got off the bus between Poydras Street and Lamar Street. Due to redevelopment, Poydras no longer exists.

4. Continue to Lamar Street – ¼ block. Turn left.

5. Go on Lamar to the bus station – 2 blocks. This is where Oswald got the taxi to his rooming house.

6. Now you need to get your car to complete the rest of Oswald's escape attempt.

Insert B redrawn

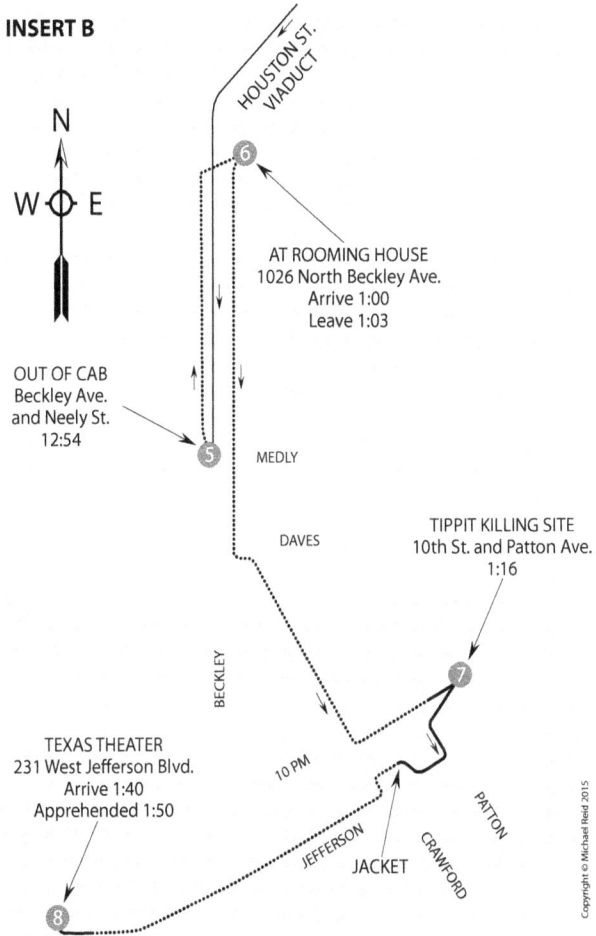

INSERT B

N
W ⊕ E

HOUSTON ST. VIADUCT

6 AT ROOMING HOUSE
1026 North Beckley Ave.
Arrive 1:00
Leave 1:03

OUT OF CAB
Beckley Ave.
and Neely St.
12:54

5

MEDLY

DAVES

TIPPIT KILLING SITE
10th St. and Patton Ave.
1:16

7

BECKLEY

TEXAS THEATER
231 West Jefferson Blvd.
Arrive 1:40
Apprehended 1:50

10 PM

PATTON

CRAWFORD

JEFFERSON

JACKET

8

Copyright © Michael Reid 2015

65

Insert B driving directions

1. Start at the Greyhound Bus Station – 205 Lamar Street (this is where Oswald got into the cab).

2. Drive toward Jackson Street (less than 1 block if you are in front of the bus station).

3. Take a right on Jackson Street.

4. Continue on Jackson Street for three blocks to S Houston.

5. Take a left on S Houston.

6. Continue on S Houston for approximately 2 miles. This will take you to the Houston Street Viaduct that crosses over the Trinity River and into the Oak Cliff neighborhood. NOTE: S Houston turns into Zang Boulevard shortly after you cross the river. Follow Zang to North Beckley.

7. Turn left on North Beckley Avenue.

8. On North Beckley go to Neely Street. This is where Oswald got out of the cab. It is 4 blocks beyond Oswald's rooming house. He apparently did not want the cab driver to know where he lived.

9. Oswald walked to his rooming house, so turn around and drive back the way you came on North Beckley to 1026 North Beckley. This was his rooming house. He went inside and got his handgun and a jacket.

10. Oswald is now walking again, so turn around one more time and proceed on North Beckley toward Neely. Go past Neely on block to E Davis Street.

11. Take a left on E Davis Street.

12. Go ½ block to N Crawford Street and take a right.

13. On N Crawford, go past 7th, 8th and 9th Streets. Proceed into the next block and stop about halfway between 9th Street and Jefferson Boulevard. At this point, Oswald took a left onto E 10th Street. E 10th Street no longer exists here due to improvements to WH Adamson High School, so you have to take a detour.

14. DETOUR FROM OSWALD'S ROUTE: Go back to E 9th Street. Take a right on 9th Street. Go 1 block to N Patton Avenue. Take a right. Go to E 10th Street.

15. At E 10th Street and N Patton Avenue, you are back on Oswald's route. This is close to where Oswald shot Tippit. An historical marker is at the site.

16. On N Patton, go one block to E Jefferson Boulevard. Take a right on E Jefferson.

17. Shortly after moving on to E Jefferson, Oswald takes off his jacket and leaves it in a used car lot. He then proceeds down Jefferson to the Texas Theater. This is almost 6 blocks from N Patton.

18. Go to the Texas Theater at 231 W Jefferson Boulevard. Oswald hid in the theater and was apprehended by the Dallas police shortly thereafter.

The Greyhound Bus Station – 205 Lamar Street

After trying and failing to get away from the crime scene on a city bus, Oswald got a cab at the bus station. He took the cab to his rooming house where he got his handgun. The bus station is still there.

www.roadarch.com

Warren Commission testimony of the cabbie [William Whaley] who gave Oswald a ride out of downtown to his rooming house...

Mr. BALL. Let's take the 12:30 trip, tell me about that, what the passenger said.

Mr. WHALEY. He said, "May I have the cab?" I said, "You sure can. Get in." And instead of opening the back door he opened the front door, which is allowable there, and got in.

Mr. BALL. Got in the front door?

Mr. WHALEY. Yes, sir. The front seat. And about that time an old lady, I think she was an old lady, I don't remember nothing but her sticking her head down past him in the door and said, "Driver, will you call me a cab down here?" She had seen him get this cab and she wanted one, too, and he opened the door a little bit like he was going to get out and he said, "I will let you have this one," and she says, "No, the driver can call me one." So, I didn't call one because I knew before I could call one would come around the block and keep it pretty well covered.

Mr. BALL. Is that what you said?

Mr. WHALEY. No, sir; that is not what I said, but that is the reason I didn't call one at the time and I asked him where he wanted to go. And he said, "500 North Beckley." Well, I started up, I started to that address, and the police cars, the sirens was going, running crisscrossing everywhere, just a big uproar in that end of town and I said, "What the hell. I wonder what the hell is the uproar?" And he never said anything. So I figured he was one of these people that don't like to talk so I never said any more to him. But when I got pretty close to 500 block at Neely and North Beckley which is the 500 block, he said, "This will do fine," and I pulled over to the curb right there. He gave me a dollar bill, the trip was 95 cents. He gave me a dollar bill and didn't say anything, just got out and closed the door and walked around the front of the cab over to the other side of the street. Of course, traffic was moving through there and I put it in gear and moved on, that is the last I saw of him.

Tippit murder scene
East 10th Street and Patton

J.D. TIPPIT

SLAIN IN THE LINE OF DUTY WHILE ON ALERT FOR PRESIDENT JOHN F. KENNEDY'S ASSASSIN, J. D. TIPPIT (1924-1963) GREW UP ON HIS FAMILY'S FARM NEAR THIS SITE. HE SERVED AS A PARATROOPER IN THE 17TH AIRBORNE DIVISION DURING WORLD WAR II AND RECEIVED THE BRONZE STAR. J.D. MARRIED HIS HIGH SCHOOL SWEETHEART IN 1946 AND STARTED A FAMILY IN RED RIVER COUNTY. HE JOINED THE DALLAS POLICE DEPARTMENT IN 1952 AND LATER WAS HONORED FOR HIS QUICK THINKING AND OUTSTANDING JUDGMENT. ON NOVEMBER 22, 1963, TIPPIT WAS WORKING A BEAT IN CENTRAL OAK CLIFF WHEN HE STOPPED LEE HARVEY OSWALD FOR QUESTIONING. OSWALD SHOT AND KILLED HIM. J.D. TIPPIT, WHO LEFT A WIFE AND THREE CHILDREN, IS BURIED AT LAUREL LAND MEMORIAL PARK IN DALLAS.

(2001)

www.cemeteries-of-tx.com

Office J.D. Tippit stopped Lee Harvey Oswald close to the corner of East 10th Avenue and Patton Avenue. This was approximately 45 minutes after President Kennedy was fatally wounded. Oswald shot Tippit four times, the final shot at close range and into the officer's right temple.

Tippit was married with three children. The site went unrecognized until November 2012 when a state historical market was placed there.

J.D. Tippit's family

www.dailymail.co.uk

Warren Commission testimony of Helen Markham, witness to the murder of Tippit...
Mr. BALL. Did you see any man walking at that time?
Mrs. MARKHAM. Yes; I seen this man on the opposite side, across the street from me. He was almost across Patton Street.
...

Mr. BALL. What did you notice then?

Mrs. MARKHAM. Well, I noticed a police car coming.

Mr. BALL. Where was the police car when you first saw it?

Mrs. MARKHAM. He was driving real slow, almost up to this man, well, say this man, and he kept, this man kept walking, you know, and the police car going real slow now, real slow, and they just kept coming into the curb, and finally they got way up there a little ways up, well, it stopped.

Mr. BALL. The police car stopped?

Mrs. MARKHAM. Yes, sir.

Mr. BALL. What about the man? Was he still walking?

Mrs. MARKHAM. The man stopped.

Mr. BALL. Then what did you see the man do?

Mrs. MARKHAM. I saw the man come over to the car very slow, leaned and put his arms just like this, he leaned over in this window and looked in this window.

Mr. BALL. He put his arms on the window ledge?

Mrs. MARKHAM. The window was down.

Mr. BALL. It was?

Mrs. MARKHAM. Yes, sir.

Mr. BALL. Put his arms on the window ledge?

Mrs. MARKHAM. On the ledge of the window.

Mr. BALL. And the policeman was sitting where?

Mrs. MARKHAM. On the driver's side.

Mr. BALL. He was sitting behind the wheel?

Mrs. MARKHAM. Yes, sir.

Mr. BALL. Was he alone in the car?

Mrs. MARKHAM. Yes.

Mr. BALL. Then what happened?

Mrs. MARKHAM. Well, I didn't think nothing about it; you know, the police are nice and friendly, and I thought friendly conversation. Well, I looked, and there were cars coming, so I had to wait. Well, in a few minutes this man made--

Mr. BALL. What did you see the policeman do?

Mrs. MARKHAM. See the policeman? Well, this man, like I told you, put his arms up, leaned over, he just a minute, and he drew back and he stepped back about two steps. Mr. Tippit--

Mr. BALL. The policeman?

Mrs. MARKHAM. The policeman calmly opened the car door, very slowly, wasn't angry or nothing, he calmly crawled out of this car, and I still just thought a friendly conversation, maybe disturbance in the house, I did not know; well, just as the policeman got--

Mr. BALL. Which way did he walk?

Mrs. MARKHAM. Towards the front of the car. And just as he had gotten even with the wheel on the driver's side--

Mr. BALL. You mean the left front wheel?

Mrs. MARKHAM. Yes; this man shot the policeman.

Mr. BALL. You heard the shots, did you?

Mrs. MARKHAM. Yes, sir.

Mr. BALL. How many shots did you hear?

Mrs. MARKHAM. Three.

Mr. BALL. What did you see the policeman do?

Mrs. MARKHAM. He fell to the ground, and his cap went a little ways out on the street.

Mr. BALL. What did the man do?

Mrs. MARKHAM. The man, he just walked calmly, fooling with his gun.

Mr. BALL. Toward what direction did he walk?

Mrs. MARKHAM. Come back towards me, turned around, and went back.

Mr. BALL. Toward Patton?

Mrs. MARKHAM. Yes, sir; towards Patton. He didn't run. It just didn't scare him to death. He didn't run. When he saw me he looked at me, stared at me. I put my hands over my face like this, closed my eyes. I gradually opened my fingers like this, and I opened my eyes, and when I did he started off in kind of a little trot.

The Texas Theater
231 West Jefferson Boulevard

AP Photo/LM Otero

The Texas Theatre is a movie theater in the Oak Cliff neighborhood of Dallas. It opened in 1931 and was part of a chain of theaters owned by Howard Hughes. Fleeing from the police after shooting Officer J.D. Tippit, Oswald hid in the theater and was arrested there. The movie playing at the time was *War is Hell*, a Korean war film starring Audie Murphy.

In 1995, the theater was nearly destroyed by fire. It sat empty and open to the elements for several years. In 2001, the Oak Cliff Foundation purchased the theater and received $1.6 million grant from the Dallas Neighborhood Renaissance Partnership for renovations. Theater management will happily give you a tour (assuming a movie is not showing). Contact them at info@aviationcinemas.com. Suggested donations are $10 for individual tours or $20 for a group.

Inside the Texas Theater

Left: A police officer points to the seat in the Texas Theatre where Lee Oswald was sitting when he was apprehended (photo taken in 1963). Dallas Police Department John F. Kennedy Collection. Right: An employee of the Texas Theater poses for a photograph at the same location where Lee Harvey Oswald was arrested (photo taken in 2013). REUTERS/Dallas Police Department/Dallas Municipal Archives.

Testimony of Dallas policeman M.N. McDonald to the Warren Commission. McDonald helped arrest Oswald at the Texas Theater.

Mr. BALL - You went down to the Texas Theatre?

Mr. McDONALD - Yes, sir.

...

Mr. BALL - What did you do?

Mr. McDONALD - Well, when I got to the front of the theater there was several police cars already at the scene, and I surmised that officers were already inside the theater. So I decided to go to the rear, in the alley, and seal off the rear. I parked my squad car. I noticed there were three or four other officers standing outside with shotguns guarding the rear exits. There were three other officers at the rear door. I joined them. We walked into the rear exit door over the alley.... And as we got inside the door, we were met by a man that was in civilian clothes, a suit, and he told us that the man that acted suspiciously as he ran into the theater was sitting downstairs in the orchestra seats, and not in the balcony. He was sitting at the rear of the theater alone. Officer Walker and I went to the exit curtains that is to the left of the movie screen. I looked into the audience. I saw the person that the shoe store salesman had pointed out to us.

Mr. BALL - Were the lights on or off?

Mr. McDONALD - The lights were up, and the movie was playing at this time.

Mr. BALL - And could you see to the rear of the theater?

Mr. McDONALD - Yes, sir.

Mr. BALL - You could see the man. Did the civilian point out to you the man in one of the rear seats?

Mr. McDONALD - He didn't point out personally. He was pointing out the suspect to another officer with him on the right of the stage, just right of the movie screen.

Mr. BALL - What did you do then?

Mr. McDONALD - Well, after seeing him, I noticed the other people in the theater--there was approximately 10 or 15 other people seated throughout the theater. There were two men sitting in the center, about 10 rows from the front. I walked up the left center aisle into the row behind these two men, and Officer C. T. Walker was behind me. When I got to these two men, I told them to get on their feet. They got up. I searched them for a weapon. I looked over my shoulder and the suspect that had been pointed out to me. He remained seated without moving, just looking at me.

Mr. BALL - Why did you frisk these two men in the center of the theater?

Mr. McDONALD - I wanted to make sure that I didn't pass anything or miss anybody. I wanted to make sure I didn't overlook anybody or anything.

Mr. BALL - And you still kept your eye on the suspect?

Mr. McDONALD - Yes, sir. He was to my back. I was looking over my shoulder at him.

Mr. BALL - Was he sitting nearest the right or the left aisle as you came in?

Mr. McDONALD - The right center aisle. He was in the second seat.

Mr. BALL - What did you do then?

Mr. McDONALD - After I was satisfied that these two men were not armed or had a weapon on them, I walked out of this row, up to the right center aisle toward the suspect. And as I walked up there, just at a normal gait, I didn't look directly at him, but I kept my eye on him and any other persons. And to my left was another man and I believe a woman was with him. But he was further back than the suspect. And just as I got to the row where the suspect was sitting, I stopped abruptly, and turned in and told him to get on his feet. He rose immediately, bringing up both hands. He got this hand about shoulder high, his left hand shoulder high, and he got his right hand about breast high. He said, "Well, it is all over now." As he said this, I put my left hand on his waist and then his hand went to the waist. And this hand struck me between the eyes on the bridge of the nose.

Mr. BALL - Did he cock his fist?

Mr. McDONALD - Yes, sir; knocking my cap off.

Mr. BALL - Which fist did he hit you with?

Mr. McDONALD - His left fist.

Mr. BALL - What happened then?

Mr. McDONALD - Well, whenever he knocked my hat off, any normal reaction was for me to go at him with this hand. Mr. BALL - Right hand?

Mr. McDONALD - Yes. I went at him with this hand, and I believe I struck him on the face, but I don't know where. And with my hand, that was on his hand over the pistol.

Mr. BALL - Did you feel the pistol?

Mr. McDONALD - Yes, sir.

Mr. BALL - Which hand was--was his right hand or his left hand on the pistol?

Mr. McDONALD - His right hand was on the pistol.

Mr. BALL - And which of your hands?

Mr. McDONALD - My left hand, at this point.

Mr. BALL - And had he withdrawn the pistol

Mr. McDONALD - He was drawing it as I put my hand.

Mr. BALL - From his waist?

Mr. McDONALD - Yes, sir.

Mr. BALL - What happened then?

Mr. McDONALD - Well, whenever I hit him, we both fell into the seats. While we were struggling around there, with this hand on the gun--

Mr. BALL - Your left hand?

Mr. McDONALD - Yes, sir. Somehow I managed to get this hand in the action also.

Mr. BALL - Your right hand?

Mr. McDONALD - Yes, sir. Now, as we fell into the seats, I called out, "I have got him," and Officer T. A. Hutson, he came to the row behind us and grabbed Oswald around the neck. And then Officer C. T. Walker came into the row that we were in and grabbed his left arm. And Officer Ray Hawkins came to the row in front of us and grabbed him from the front. By the time all three of these officers had got there, I had gotten my right hand on the butt of the pistol and jerked it free.

Mr. BALL - Had you felt any movement of the hammer?

Mr. McDONALD - Yes, sir. When this hand--we went down into the seats.

Mr. BALL - When your left hand went into the seats, what happened?

Mr. McDONALD - It felt like something had grazed across my hand. I felt movement there. And that was the only movement I felt. And I heard a snap. I didn't know what it was at the time.

Mr. BALL - Was the pistol out of his waist at that time?

Mr. McDONALD - Yes, sir.

Mr. BALL - Do you know any way it was pointed?

Mr. McDONALD - Well, I believe the muzzle was toward me, because the sensation came across this way. To make a movement like that, it would have to be the cylinder or the hammer.

Mr. BALL - Across your left palm?

Mr. McDONALD - Yes, sir. And my hand was directly over the pistol in this manner. More or less the butt. But not on the butt.

Mr. BALL - What happened when you jerked the pistol free?

Mr. McDONALD - When I jerked it free, I was down in the seats with him, with my head, some reason or other, I don't know why, and when I brought the pistol out, it grazed me across the cheek here, and I put it all the way out to the aisle, holding it by the butt. I gave the pistol to Detective Bob Carroll at that point.

Mr. BALL - Grazed your left cheek?

Mr. McDONALD - Yes, sir.

Mr. BALL - Scratched--noticeable scratch?

Mr. McDONALD - Yes, sir; about a 4-inch scratch just above the eye to just above the lip.

Mr. BALL - Then what happened after that?

Mr. McDONALD - Well, the officers that had come to my aid started handcuffing him and taking him out of the theater.

Mr. BALL - What did he say--anything?

Mr. McDONALD - Well, he was cursing a little bit and hollering police brutality, for one thing.

Testimony of C.T. Walker, Dallas Police Officer. Walker escorted Oswald out of the Texas Theater after his arrest.

Mr. BELIK. In any event, you brought him down the lobby of the theatre?

Mr. WALKEK. When we went out the front door, he started hollering, "I protest this police brutality." People out there were hollering, "Kill the s.0.b." "Let us have him. We want him." Mr. BELIN. At that time, did anyone connect him with the assassination of the President?

Mr. WALKER. Not unless the crowd had assumed that is who we were after, I don't know.

Mr. BELIN. When you were after him, you were after him for what?

Mr. WALKER. For the killing of Officer Tippit.

Oswald is custody outside the Texas Theater

en.wikipedia.org

Dallas Municipal Building
106 S. Harwood

After shooting President Kennedy and Officer Tippit, Lee Harvey Oswald was arrested and jailed in the Municipal Building. Two days later he was fatally shot by Jack Ruby in the basement garage of that building. The building housed municipal offices and the police department and jail until the late 1970's. It still houses the Municipal Court. Oswald-related locations in the building are not publically accessible.

"Dallas - Municipal Building 01A" by Joe Mabel. Licensed under CC BY-SA 3.0 via Wikimedia Commons -http://commons.wikimedia.org/wiki/File:Dallas

Below is the entrance to the underground garage in the Dallas Municipal Building. Jack Ruby entered the building through this entrance and seconds later shot Oswald.

jfk50geotrail.com

Below: The bottom of the garage entrance. This is where Jack Ruby shot Oswald.

AP Photo/LM Otero

Below: Jack Ruby shooting Oswald

AP Photo/LM Otero

Below: The cell in the Dallas Municipal Building that held Lee Harvey Oswald. The cell is not accessible to the public.

AP Photo/LM Otero

Testimony of Jack Ruby to the Warren Commission. His testimony is given to Chief Justice Earl Warren of the Supreme Court.

Mr. RUBY... When I left my apartment that morning----

Chief Justice WARREN. What morning?

Mr. RUBY. Sunday morning.

Chief Justice WARREN. Sunday morning.

Mr. RUBY. Let's go back. Saturday I watched Rabbi Seligman. Any of you watch it that Saturday morning?

Chief Justice WARREN. No; I didn't happen to hear it.

Mr. RUBY. He went ahead and eulogized that here is a man that fought in every battle, went to every country, and had to come back to his own country to be shot in the back [starts crying]. I must be a great actor, I tell you that.

Chief Justice WARREN. No.

Mr. RUBY. That created a tremendous emotional feeling for me, the way he said that. Prior to all the other times, I was carried away. Then that Saturday night, I didn't do anything but visit a little club over here and had a Coca-Cola, because I was sort of depressed. A fellow that owns the Pago Club, Bob Norton, and he knew something was wrong with me in the certain mood I was in. And I went home and that weekend, the Sunday morning, and saw a letter to Caroline, two columns about a 16-inch area. Someone had written a letter to Caroline. The most heartbreaking letter. I don't remember the contents. Do you remember that?

Mr. MOORE. I think I saw it.

Mr. RUBY. Yes; and alongside that letter on the same sheet of paper was a small comment in the newspaper that, I don't know how it was stated, that Mrs. Kennedy may have to come back for the trial of Lee Harvey Oswald. That caused me to go like I did; that caused me to go like I did. I don't know, Chief Justice, but I got so carried away. And I remember prior to that thought, there has never been another thought in my mind; I was never malicious toward this person. No one else requested me to do anything. I never spoke to anyone about attempting to do anything. No subversive organization gave me any idea. No underworld person made any effort to contact me. It all happened that Sunday morning. The last thing I read was that Mrs. Kennedy may have to come back to Dallas for trial for Lee Harvey Oswald, and, I don't know what bug got ahold of me. I don't know what it is, but I am going to tell the truth word for word. I am taking a pill called Preludin. It is a harmless pill, and it is very easy to get in the drugstore. It isn't a highly prescribed pill. I use it for dieting. I don't partake of that much food. I think that was a stimulus to give me an emotional feeling that suddenly I felt, which was so stupid, that I wanted to show my love for our faith, being of the Jewish faith, and I never used the term and I don't want to go into that--suddenly the feeling, the emotional feeling came within me that someone owed this debt to our beloved President to save her the ordeal of coming back. I don't know why that came through my mind. And I drove past Main Street, past the County Building, and there was a crowd already gathered there. And I guess I thought I knew he was going to be moved at 10 o'clock, I don't know. I listened to the radio; and I passed a crowd and it looked--I am repeating myself--and I took it for granted he had already been moved. And I parked my car in the lot across from the Western Union. Prior to that, I got a call from a little girl--she wanted-some money--that-worked for me, and I said, "Can't you wait till payday?" And she said, "Jack, you are going to be closed." So my purpose was to go to the Western Union--my double purpose but the thought of doing, committing the act wasn't until I left my apartment. Sending the wire was when I had the phone call--or the money order. I drove down Main Street--there was a little incident I left out, that I started to go down a driveway, but I wanted to go by the wreaths, and I saw them and started to cry again. Then I drove, parked the car across from the Western Union, went into the Western Union, sent the money order, whatever it was, walked the distance from the Western Union to the ramp--I didn't sneak in. I didn't linger in there. I didn't crouch or hide behind anyone, unless the television camera can make it seem that way. There was an officer talking--I don't know what rank he had--talking to a Sam Pease in a car parked up on the curb. I walked down those few steps, and there was the person that--I wouldn't say I saw red--it was a feeling I had for our beloved President and Mrs. Kennedy, that he was insignificant to what my purpose was. And when I walked down the ramp--I would say there was an 8-foot clearance--not that I wanted to be a hero, or I didn't realize that even if the officer would have observed me, the klieg lights, but I can't take that. I did not mingle with the crowd. There was no one near me when I walked down that ramp, because if you will time the time I sent the money order, I think it was 10:17 Sunday morning. I think the actual act was committed--I take that back--was it 11 o'clock? You should know this.

Mr. MOORE. 11: 21.

Mr. RUBY. No; when Oswald was shot.

Mr. MOORE. I understood it to be 11:22.

Mr. RUBY. The clock stopped and said 11:21. I was watching on that thing; yes. Then it must have been 11:17, closer to 18. That is the timing when I left the Western Union to the time of the bottom of the ramp. You wouldn't have time enough to have any conspiracy, to be self-saving, to mingle with the crowd, as it was told about me. I realize it is a terrible thing I have done, and it was a stupid thing, but I just was carried away emotionally. Do you follow that?

Chief Justice WARREN. Yes; I do indeed, every word.

Mr. RUBY. I had the gun in my right hip pocket, and impulsively, if that is the correct word here, I saw him, and that is all I can say. And I didn't care what happened to me. I think I used the words, "You killed my President, you rat." The next thing, I was down on the floor. I said, "I am Jack Ruby. You all know me." I never used anything malicious, nothing like s.o.b. I never said that I wanted to get three more off, as they stated. The only words, and I was highly emotional; to Ray Hall--he interrogated more than any other person down there--all I believe I said to him was, "I didn't want Mrs. Kennedy to come back to trial." And I forget what else. And I used a little expression like being of the Jewish faith, I wanted to show that we love our President, even though we are not of the same faith. And I have a friend of mine do you mind if it is a slipshod story?

Chief Justice WARREN. No; you tell us in your own way.

Mr. RUBY. A fellow whom I sort of idolized is of the Catholic faith, and a gambler. Naturally in my business you meet people of various backgrounds. And the thought came, we were very close, and I always thought a lot of him, and I knew that Kennedy, being Catholic, I knew how heartbroken he was, and even his picture of this Mr. McWillie flashed across me, because I have a great fondness for him. All that blended into the thing that, like a screwball, the way it turned out, that I thought that I would sacrifice myself for the few moments of saving Mrs. Kennedy the discomfiture-of coming back to trial. Now all these things of my background, I should have been the last person in the world to want to be a martyr. It happens, doesn't it, Chief Warren?

Parkland Hospital
5201 Harry Hines Blvd

Oswald's second child was born at Parkland. President Kennedy, Lee Harvey Oswald and Jack Ruby were all pronounced dead at Parkland.

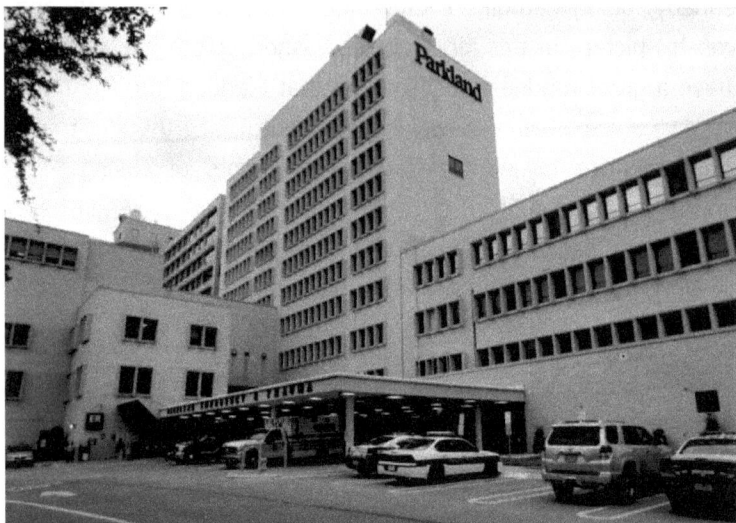

Testimony of Dr. Robert McClelland, a physician who treated President Kennedy when he was brought into Parkland after being shot by Oswald....

Mr. SPECTER - What did you observe as to President Kennedy's condition at that time?

Dr. McCLELLAND - Well, on initially coming into the room and inspecting him from a distance of only 2 or 3 feet as I put on a pair of surgical gloves, it was obvious that he had sustained a probably mortal head injury, and that his face was extremely swollen and suffused with blood appeared cyanotic

Mr. SPECTER - "Cyanotic"---may I interrupt-just what do you mean by that in lay terms?

Dr. McCLELLAND - This mean bluish discoloration, bluish-black discoloration of the tissue. The eyes were somewhat protuberant, which is usually seen after massive head injuries denoting increased intracranial pressure, and it seemed that he perhaps was not making, at the time at least, spontaneous respiratory movements, but was receiving artificial respiration from a machine, an anesthesia machine.

Mr. SPECTER - Who was operating that machine?

Dr. McCLELLAND - The machine---there was a changeover, just as I came in, one of the doctors in the room, I don't recall which one, had been operating what we call an intermittent positive pressure breathing machine.

.....

Mr. SPECTER - What did you observe, if anything, as to the status of the neck wound when you first arrived?

Dr. McCLELLAND - The neck wound, when I first arrived, was at this time converted into a tracheotomy incision. The skin incision had been made by Dr. Perry, and he told me---although I did not see that---that he had made the incision through a very small, perhaps less than one quarter inch in diameter wound in the neck.

Mr. SPECTER - Do you recall whether he described it any more precisely than that?

Dr. McCLELLAND - He did not at that time.

Mr. SPECTER - Has he ever described it any more precisely for you?

Dr. McCLELLAND - He has since that time.

Mr. SPECTER - And what description has he given of it since that time?

Dr. McCLELLAND - As well as I can recall, the description that he gave was essentially as I have just described, that it was a very small injury, with clear cut, although somewhat irregular margins of less than a quarter inch in diameter, with minimal tissue damage surrounding it on the skin.

Mr. SPECTER - Now, was there anything left for you to observe of that bullet wound, or had the incision obliterated it?

Dr. McCLELLAND - The incision had obliterated it, essentially, the skin portion, that is.

Mr. SPECTER - Before proceeding to describe what you did in connection with the tracheostomy, will you more fully describe your observation with respect to the head wound?

Dr. McCLELLAND - As I took the position at the head of the table that I have already described, to help out with the tracheotomy, I was in such a position that I could very closely examine the head wound, and I noted that the right posterior portion of the skull had been extremely blasted. It had been shattered, apparently, by the force of the shot so that the parietal bone was protruded up through the scalp and seemed to be fractured almost along its right posterior half, as well as some of the occipital bone being fractured in its lateral haft, and this sprung open the bones that I mentioned in such a way that you could actually look down into the skull cavity itself and see that probably a third or so, at least, of the brain tissue, posterior cerebral tissue and some of the cerebellar tissue had been blasted out. There was a large amount of bleeding which was occurring mainly from the large venous channels in the skull which had been blasted open.

Mr. SPECTER - Was he alive at the time you first saw him?

Dr. McCLELLAND - I really couldn't say, because as I mentioned in the hectic activity---I really couldn't say what his blood pressure was or what his pulse was or anything of that sort. The only thing I could say that would perhaps give evidence---this is not vital activity---at most, is that maybe he made one or two spontaneous respiratory movements but it would be difficult to say, since the machine was being used on him, whether these were true spontaneous respirations or not.

.....

Mr. SPECTER - What effect did this medical treatment have on President Kennedy?

Dr. McCLELLAND - As near as we could tell, unfortunately, none. We felt that from the time we saw him, most of us agreed, all of us agreed rather, that this was a mortal wound, but that in spite of this feeling that all attempts possible should be made to revive him, as far as establishing the airway breathing for him, and replacing blood and what not, but unfortunately the loss of blood and the loss of cerebral and cerebellar tissues were so great that the efforts were of no avail.

Mr. SPECTER - Was he conscious at that time that you saw him?

Dr. McCLELLAND - No.

Mr. SPECTER - And, at what time did he expire?

Dr. McCLELLAND - He was pronounced dead at 1 p.m. on November 22.

Mr. SPECTER - What was the cause of death in your opinion?

Dr. McCLELLAND - The cause of death, I would say, would be massive head injuries with loss of large amounts of cerebral and cerebellar tissues and massive blood loss.

Below: The trauma center where President Kennedy was pronounced dead no longer exists. There is, however, a simple plaque commemorating the day President Kennedy died.

ORIGINAL SITE
TRAUMA 1
NOVEMBER 22, 1963

Shannon Rose Hill Memorial Park.
7301 E. Lancaster Ave. Fort Worth.

Oswald is buried in Shannon Rose Hill Memorial Park in Fort Worth. The Oswald family has requested the cemetery not provide directions to the grave. But here is how to find it...

- From E. Lancaster Ave./Hwy 180 turn north onto Rose Hill Drive.
- Take the first right into the cemetery.
- Take the first right. This path parallels Rose Hill Drive. There is a red mausoleum ahead.
- Park at the mausoleum.
- Walk to the west (back toward Rose Hill Drive). Oswald's plain marker is a couple of rows in. Nick Beef's marker is beside Oswald's.

According to the *New York Times* (August 10, 2013) Nick Beef is actually a man named Patric Abedin. He bought the plot and marker in 1996 because he felt he had a personal connection to JFK, having met him the day before he was shot. Abedin has no plans to be buried beside Oswald.

In 1981, Oswald's body was exhumed. As the New York Times explains it... "DALLAS, Oct. 4— The body resting in Lee Harvey Oswald's coffin was removed from its grave today, and a team of examining pathologists said that the remains were indeed Oswald's. The finding appeared to end speculation that the corpse might have been that of a Russian agent sent here to kill President Kennedy in 1963." *Oswald's body is exhumed; an autopsy affirms identity*, New York Times. October 5, 1981

www.twincities.com

The Ozzie Rabbit Lodge
6463 E Lancaster Ave, Fort Worth.

The Lodge is near Shannon Rose Hill Memorial Park. It is named after Oswald's Marine nickname – Ozzie Rabbit. The walls in the bar are covered with Oswald art and articles.

threeshotswerefired.com

Review on Yelp

"I'm standing outside trying to figure out what exactly am I looking at. Is that Oswald, as in Lee Harvey, wearing bunny ears? It most definitely is. Rumor has it that he is buried somewhere around here... The name of the bar comes from the fact that in the Army Oswald's call sign was "Rabbit" after a Disney Cartoon Rabbit. This was because he was so small." Chris E, Austin, Texas. 5/2/2009. Yelp.

The JFK Memorial in Dallas
646 Main Street

commons.wikimedia.org

This memorial to President Kennedy is in downtown Dallas close to where the President was assassinated. The Memorial is an "open tomb" symbolizing the freedom of President Kennedy's spirit.

There has been some controversy regarding the memorial. Architectural critic Witold Rybczynski said the memorial is "poorly done" and that President Kennedy "deserved better."

Timeline – Jack Ruby (born Jacob Leon Rubenstein on March 25, 1911)

Dallas Police Department photo

Jack Ruby was the nightclub operator in Dallas who shot Lee Oswald. A jury trial found Ruby guilty of murdering Oswald and sentenced him to be executed. Ruby appealed the conviction and was granted a new trial, but died before it could be held.

Ruby's life before Dallas. 1911 – 1947 (36 years)

- Born Jacob Rubenstein in Chicago on March 25, 1911.
- His father was a violent alcoholic. His mother suffered from "psychoneuroses" and died in a mental hospital.

- As a child, Ruby was arrested for truancy and spent time at the Institute of Juvenile Research (part of the psychiatry department of the University of Illinois Chicago). According to the report by the Institute, Ruby was quick-tempered, disobedient and egocentric.

- When released from the Institute, Ruby lived in a number of foster homes.

- As a youth, Ruby scalped tickets and sold novelty items.

- Ruby lived in Los Angeles and San Francisco with several friends 1933 – 1937. In Los Angeles, he was a singing waiter and sold tip sheets at Santa Anita Race Track. In San Francisco, he sold newspaper subscriptions door to door.

- Returning to Chicago, Ruby was employed by Local 20467 of the Scrap Iron and Junk Handlers Union from late 1937 to early 1940. He also sold novelties and gambling devices known as punchboards.

- He was drafted in 1943 and served an aircraft mechanic in the Army Air Forces during World War II.

- In April 1944, his mother died.

Jack Ruby in Dallas (1947 – January 1967 (19 years)
- In 1947, Ruby moved to Dallas to help his sister Eva Grant run the Singapore Supper Club in which Ruby was an investor.

- In December 1947, Ruby, along with his brothers, changed their last name from Rubenstein to Ruby.

- While in Dallas, Ruby's primary occupation was running nightclubs and dancehalls.

- In 1952, Ruby experienced financial difficulties and lost both of the clubs he owned at the time – the Silver Spur and Bob Wills Ranch House.

- Subsequently, Ruby operated the Vegas Club and the Sovereign Club. Ruby's sister ran the Vegas Club and Ruby the Sovereign, changing its name to the Carousel. The Carousel was one of several downtown strip clubs.

- Ruby's employees at the Carousel say he had a violent temper and frequently got into physical altercations, although he cared about the people who worked for him. He regularly fired people and then shortly thereafter rehired them.

- Ruby dealt on a cash basis. He carried the money on himself and in the trunk of his car and paid some bills with cashier's checks. When he carried cash, he also carried a gun.

- Ruby was delinquent on his personal and excise taxes. At the time of his arrest in 1963, he owed the Federal government over $40,000 in back taxes (about $300,000 in 2015 dollars).

- Besides operating his nightclubs, Ruby was involved in a number of speculative businesses including selling pizza crusts to restaurants, manufacturing a vitamin formula, building resort cabins at a local lake and selling stainless steel razor blades. None of these enterprises were particularly successful.

- Ruby was friendly with mob-related people and professional gamblers.

- For more than 11 years, Ruby dated Alice Nichols, a secretary at a life insurance company.

- Ruby had poor credit and often seemed to be strapped for cash. In 1959, however, his net income was a little over $14,000 (about $108,000 in 2015 dollars).

November 22 - 23: The assassination of Kennedy

- Ruby was in the advertising office of the *Dallas Morning News* when he first heard of the assassination of President Kennedy.

- Out of respect for the Kennedy family, Ruby closed the Carousel Club for the night.

- He was seen in Dallas Police Headquarters at different times after Oswald's arrest. Newsreel footage shows Ruby impersonating a newspaper reporter during a press conference at Dallas Police Headquarters.

November 24: Ruby shoots Oswald

- The Dallas Chief of Police told the press corps that Oswald would be transferred to another jail at 10:00 AM.

- Ruby was still at home at 10:00 AM. Shortly after ten, Ruby received a call from one of his dancers asking him to wire money to her.

· Ruby dressed and went to the Western Union close to police headquarters. Leaving his dog in the car, he wired the money at 11:17 AM. Then Ruby walked up the alley, passed through a crowd gathered at the police station and entered the garage ramp to the building.

- Ruby got to the bottom of the ramp at the very moment Oswald was being escorted to a vehicle in the underground garage. Ruby stepped forward and shot Oswald. It was three or four minutes since he had wired the money.

Below: Oswald stepping forward to shoot Oswald.

Photograph by Jack Beers Jr., Dallas Morning News photographer. Ruby about to shoot Oswald

Aftermath

- March 14, 1964. At trial, Ruby was found guilty of "murder with malice" and sentenced to die in the electric chair. It was the first courtroom verdict to be televised in U.S. history.

- The Texas Court of Criminal Appeals ruled on October 5, 1966 that the refusal of the court to grant a change of venue made it impossible for Ruby to obtain a fair trial.

- Arrangements were being made for a new trial to be held in in Wichita Falls, Texas. Before the new trial could begin, however, Ruby died of a pulmonary embolism, a complication of lung cancer (January 3, 1967). The autopsy showed he had 15 brain tumors.

Ruby lived here
1719 ½ South Ervay Street

Ruby rented an apartment here in 1955. The building used to house the Nugrape Bottling Company. During prohibition, Nugrape produced a grape flavored drink. The building's second story was completed in 1932.

texashideout.tripod.com

Ruby lived here
3929 Rawlins

Ruby lived in an apartment at 3929 Rawlins in 1956. This building is currently called the Rawlins Chateau Apartments.

www.apartmentsearch.com

Ruby lived here
500 North Marsalis

Ruby moved into the dwelling in March 1962. He lived here from March until November 1962 at which point he moved to 223 South Ewing.

Google

Bob Wills' Ranch House
216 Corinth St

The Ranch House was started by the "King of Western Swing," Bob Wills. Experiencing financial problems, Wills sold the Ranch House to Jack Ruby and partners in 1952. Ruby in turn sold it to someone else. Subsequent to Ruby owning it, the club was renamed the Longhorn Ballroom. In the 1950's and 60's, it was a Dallas hotspot for performers like George Jones, Merle Haggard, Ray Price and Loretta Lynn. The Longhorn is still operating as a music venue and country western dance hall.

A postcard showing Bob Wills Ranch House

The Longhorn Ballroom

Alice Nichols, Jack Ruby's girlfriend

"The only 'decent' woman in Jack Ruby's life was Alice Nichols, a shy widow who worked for an insurance company. He dated her on and off for eleven years. The reason Ruby couldn't marry Alice, he told many of his friends, was that he had made his mother a deathbed promise that he wouldn't marry a gentile. Ruby's mother had died in an insane asylum in Chicago." *Who Was Jack Ruby? How a Small-Time Strip Club Operator Ushered in America's Age of Violence*, by Gary Cartwright in Texas Monthly, November 1975.

Testimony of Alice Nichols to the Warren Commission...

Mrs. NICHOLS... I started going with him [Jack Ruby] the latter part of 1949, and I don't remember the exact date. It was several months after I first saw him before I ever went with him. I would say it was 1948, winter of 1948 and 1949, somewhere in there.

.....

Mr. GRIFFIN. How would you describe Jack in terms of his impressions and what he would look forward to and the kind of things he liked?

Mrs. NICHOLS. Well, I think that Jack had a lot of drive. He was ambitious. He was always looking for some way to make money, some extra way to make money.

Mr. GRIFFIN. Was there anything in particular that attracted you to Jack? Made Jack attractive to you? Any particular quality about him?

Mrs. NICHOLS. He was very nice to me. He always treated me with respect.

Mr. GRIFFIN. Did Jack, was he the kind of person that would unburden himself to you with his personal problems and background?

Mrs. NICHOLS. Well he talked to me about some of his problems. I don't know that he talked to me about all of them, but he did discuss some of his problems with me.

Mr. GRIFFIN. What kind of problems did he seem to have?

Mrs. NICHOLS. Well, his business problems. When he lost the Bob Wills Ranch House, he discussed that with me. He was very upset about that. He lost a lot of money in that deal. He had to go back to Chicago at that time, and he discussed his business deals with me when he bought the Vegas Club.

.....

Mr. GRIFFIN. Did you feel that Jack talked to you about all of his enterprises; business activities?

Mrs. NICHOLS. Well, I knew of nothing that he didn't discuss with me. I don't know of any activities that he didn't discuss.

Mr. GRIFFIN. Well, did you feel Jack was the kind of person who might do things that he wouldn't discuss with people?

Mrs. NICHOLS. Discuss with people?

Mr. GRIFFIN. Yes; with other people who weren't involved in that particular activity?

Mrs. NICHOLS. I don't know. He always talked freely to me, I thought. I never did feel that he--Jack was a big talker. He talks a lot; quite an extrovert.

Mr. GRIFFIN. How did you happen to break up with Jack?

Mrs. NICHOLS. It was a gradual thing. We had no quarrel. We just quit. He quit calling me. We just quit going together.

The Carousel Club
1312 ½ Commerce Street (no longer there)

The Carousel was one of two clubs Ruby owned in November 1963. The other was the Vegas Club, managed by his sister Eva. At the Carousel, Ruby usually employed 4 dancers (strippers) and a master of ceremonies. "... the Carousel was strictly a clip joint where Ruby's girls hustled $1.98 bottles of champagne for whatever they could get... [usually $15 to $75]." *Who was Jack Ruby*? By Gary Cartwright in Texas Monthly, November 1975.

flashbak.com

Testimony of Andrew Armstrong, Jr., one of Ruby's employees at the Carousel Club...

Mr. HUBERT. Can you tell us what sort of man he [Jack Ruby] was?

Mr. ARMSTRONG. Worried and disturbed always.

Mr. HUBERT. Now, how did that manifest itself so that you could tell that he was worried and disturbed always?

Mr. ARMSTRONG. Now, I'll tell you this--there was always--if he was sitting down inside the club in the daytime at one of the tables and some people came in, he would always want to hold a conversation with them, he would always want to talk about something, and I have seen numbers of times when someone had said something about a certain thing, he would get angry about it without even knowing it--he would just get angry, just like that, but that would pass over in a matter of seconds.

Mr. HUBERT. When he got angry, how did he act?

Mr. ARMSTRONG. He would always let people know if they said anything that he didn't like.

Mr. HUBERT. How did he act?

Mr. ARMSTRONG. Sort of like ungentlemanlike in a nice way--let me see if I can explain it any better?

Mr. HUBERT. I wish you would.

Mr. ARMSTRONG. It was like I'll give you an example, which is the best way I can explain it.

Mr. HUBERT. All right.

Mr. ARMSTRONG. I have seen at times when he would walk up to someone that had the feet out in the aisle and the girls couldn't get by or some man doing something that he didn't have any business, like hitting the girls when they passed by, or something like that, and they would tell Jack--if he was in a certain mood or something was bothering him, he wouldn't go over and say--ask his customers who were spending money in his club, in a nice way not to do that, he would just hit him on the shoulder like this and say, "Watch it, Buddy, I don't allow that in my place"--you know--real mean like which is something that I never approved of.

Mr. HUBERT. He did that quite often?

Mr. ARMSTRONG. Quite often, and that's the way it would happen with any stranger. Now, if he knew someone, he would always hold off or get someone else to do it. If he knew somebody and they were doing something he didn't like, he would always get me or one of the girls to do it.

Mr. HUBERT. We started off this sequence of questions by your statement that he was always worried and disturbed, I think was the phrase, and you have given me that example. Weren't there some times when he was not?

Mr. ARMSTRONG. There was very few times when he was not and I always had the feeling that if he had that smile and talking and laughing, if it lasts all night, I always had the feeling that he would still have that worried and disturbed look and expression, later on after the club closed, somewhere after--I don't know-- after he got in bed or the next morning or something like that. It never lasted long.

Mr. HUBERT. You got along all right with him, didn't you?

Mr. ARMSTRONG. We got along--we was always arguing, differences of opinion and things like that.

Mr. HUBERT. Was he nasty with you?

Mr. ARMSTRONG. Not--I wouldn't say he was nasty. I would say if I didn't know him--I would say he was nasty. I would say that I would go so far as to say that he was even cruel.

Mr. HUBERT. To you?

Mr. ARMSTRONG. To me and to a lot of the employees.

112

Mr. HUBERT. Give us some examples of the cruelty you are speaking of.

Mr. ARMSTRONG. Well, you could say--we had a speaker in the corner, a high fidelity speaker over in the right-hand corner.

Mr. HUBERT. A loudspeaker?

Mr. ARMSTRONG. Yes, in the right-hand corner and it had to be turned on individually. It had to turned on or it wouldn't come over the system and it was my job to see that it was turned on every night, and there was times I was too busy and had too many things to do and forgot about it, but not that often, and if he came in--the first thing he checked was the sound. The MC was on stage and if he couldn't hear that box over there, he would come straight to me and it was like I had took half of the club away or something like that.

Mr. HUBERT. What would he say or do?

Mr. ARMSTRONG. Well, he would just get all riled up about that--he would just get all riled up about that one little incident.

Mr. HUBERT. When you say "all riled up," that's your own words of description of what he was doing, but we don't get just what his physical acts were unless you tell us. What is "riled up"? Raising his voice, cursing?

Mr. ARMSTRONG. Raising his voice.

Mr. HUBERT. Throwing his voice, throwing his arms about, hitting people, doing what?

Mr. ARMSTRONG. No, not hitting people he wouldn't ever hit anyone, but it always the impression that he might. There was always the feeling that he might.

Mr. HUBERT. Did his facial expressions change?

Mr. ARMSTRONG. Sort of like.

Mr. HUBERT. Did he curse?

Mr. ARMSTRONG. No--no more than--the only curse word that he would use more when he did use it was damn it.

Mr. HUBERT. Well, on occasions like he got all riled up, as you have told us, would it consist of calling you a fool or threatening to fire you or raising his voice, cursing you, what was it?

Mr. ARMSTRONG. Threatening to fire me would be the thing, because he fired me 50 times or 100 times.

Mr. HUBERT. Apparently you didn't stay fired.

Mr. ARMSTRONG. He threatened my job every day.

Mr. HUBERT. He threatened your job every day?

Mr. ARMSTRONG. Almost every day.

Mr. HUBERT. And then what would happen?

Mr. ARMSTRONG. Nothing--if I left he would call me back. If I left there fired, all I would have to do is come down and open the club up the next day and go on back to work.

The Adolphus Hotel
1321 Commerce Street

The Adolphus Hotel, located right across the street from where the Carousel Club used to be, was an occasional Ruby hang-out. The hotel is on the U.S. National Register of Historic Places.

www.tripadvisor.com

Lucas B&B Restaurant
3520 Oak Lawn Street

The Lucas B&B was at 3520 Oak Lawn. It was just a few doors down from Ruby's Vegas Club at 3508 Oak Lawn. Ruby dropped into Lucas B&B occasionally and was arrested there at one time for carrying a concealed weapon. The restaurant is no longer there, but the sign still is.

flickr.com

Campisi's Egyptian Restaurant
5610 E. Mockingbird Lane

Jack Ruby was a regular at Campisi's and ate there the night before he shot Lee Harvey Oswald. Joe Campisi, the owner, visited Oswald in prison after he shot Oswald.

The restaurant has been serving Italian food since 1946 and is still in the same location (although the owners have since added other locations in the Dallas area). Here is what they say on the website: "Family owned and operated for 65 years. Campisi's has been 'The' Italian Restaurant of Dallas since 1946.'" The "Egyptian" part of the name does not fit Italian food. When Mr. Campisi opened the restaurant, "the Egyptian Restaurant" sign was already in place. He could not afford to buy a new sign, so he kept the original.

www.flickr.com

117

Mr. HORNBECK. Now, a few days after Jack Ruby shot Lee Harvey Oswald you paid him a visit in jail?

MR. CAMPISI. Bill Decker who was sheriff at that time had called me and said, "Joe, Jack Ruby has said he would like to see some of his best friends, closest friends." He said, "He has your name on a list, you and Marie," who is my wife. He says, "Would you like to come up and talk to him?" I said, "Yeah, I would like to go up and visit the guy."

Mr. HORNBECK. Excuse me. Sheriff Decker told you that both your name and your wife's name was on that list?

MR. CAMPISI. Yes.

Mr. HORNBECK. Did he mention your brother's name was on that list?

MR. CAMPISI. No. No. So we went up and, I don't know whether it was on a Sunday or what day it was we went up.

Mr. HORNBECK. When you say "we", did your wife accompany you?

MR. CAMPISI. Yes. And so we go up and he is in a little cell, and there is a deputy sitting in the cell with him, so we stand there and walk up and say, "Hi, Jack." He says, "Hi, Joe. Hi, Marie. What are the people saying about me?' I said, "They are not saying nothing about you." Now, I don't whether he had said to me, but something about, he said, "Jews have got --" I think he said something about, "Well, Jews have got class. Nobody but me could do it," something like this. And so we talked, and I asked him how he felt, you know. He had just wanted to know how the people on the street, his friends, thought about what he did. I said, "They don't think nothing," you know.

.....

118

Mr. HORNBECK. ...There is also an indication that during the time that you were talking to Jack Ruby he broke down and cried.

MR. CAMPISI. I think he did cry a little bit, yes.

Mr. HORNBECK. Before we go into the comment that occasioned the crying, was crying something that would have surprised you about Jack Ruby, or was he an emotional type of person so that you would not be surprised?

MR. CAMPISI. I would, you know, think that he was feeling sorry for himself, you know.

Mr. HORNBECK. Well, my question goes to what kind of an emotional, state Jack Ruby was capable of reaching. For instance, you have indicated in his club that he apparently had a very quick temper.

MR. CAMPISI. Uh-huh.

Mr. HORNBECK. With regard to either laughing or crying was he fairly quick to change moods?

MR. CAMPISI. He was quick to hit somebody, you know. I had never seen him cry. That was the first time, you know, that we saw him cry. Now, whether he was crying there because we were there, you know, and he considered us his friends, and my respect and my wife, you know. He felt sorry for himself, you know.

The Oak Cliff neighborhood

Oak Cliff is an older, established neighborhood in Dallas. Both Oswald and Ruby lived in Oak Cliff. The Texas Theater is in Oak Cliff as well as the spot where Oswald shot Officer Tippit.

Oswald's rooming house at 1026 N Beckley was less than five minutes by car from Ruby's apartment at 223 S Ewing. Ruby's apartment was 2 – 3 minutes by car from where Oswald shot Officer Tippit and less than 5 minutes from the Texas Theater.

Oswald and Ruby both shopped at Cliff Sanitary Grocery in Oak Cliff, although the owner did not recall them ever being in the store at the same time. Oswald and Ruby both ate at Dodd's House restaurant in Oak Cliff, although none of the employees at the restaurant could remember them ever being in Dodd's at the same time.

Jefferson Avenue, Oak Cliff

www.iliveindallas.com

Cliff Sanitary Grocery
Formerly at 897 Lancaster Avenue

From the Warren Commission Report – Testimony of Sam Milkie.

Mr. Milkie is the proprietor of the Cliff Sanitary Grocery, 897 Lancaster Avenue, Oak Cliff.   The Cliff Sanitary Grocery is located approximately eleven blocks from the residence of Jack Ruby, from the Ewing Street residence of Jack Ruby and is on the route Ruby could take while commuting to and from his residence in downtown Dallas.

Miilkie has known Ruby for approximately a year as Ruby on the average has made two or three purchases a month at the Cliff Sanitary Grocery. Ruby generally stopped at the Cliff Sanitary Grocery to purchase steaks which Milkie presumed that Ruby cooked at home since he was a bachelor. On each occasion Ruby always asked Milkie for bones for his dogs. According to Milkie, Ruby spoke of his dogs "as though they were human beings." Ruby made purchases in the Cliff Sanitary Grocery on approximately three occasions in November.   The last time Ruby stopped at the Cliff Sanitary Grocery was but a few days prior to the assassination of President Kennedy.
....

Milkie also advised that Lee Harvey Oswald had also been a customer of his at the Sanitary Grocery from late October and November 1963.   Milkie stated that Oswald's residence on Beckley was but a short distance from the Cliff Sanitary Grocery Store.   To the best of Milkie's recollection, Oswald made purchases at his store on approximately three or four occasions and he feels that the last time that Oswald was in the store was approximately a week before the assassination of the President... Oswald, in making his purchases in the store, generally bought a loaf of bread, lunch meat and milk.

He specifically recalls Oswald from the method in which Oswald purchased lunch meat from him. He can recall Oswald methodically thinking the amount of food he would need for a specific period perhaps for a week and then in selecting the lunch meat Oswald always asked Milkie to remove the top slice of the stack as he did not want the top slice. Milkie stated that Oswald impressed him as a person who was very conscientious of his money and was living very frugally.

Milkie stated that at no time during the period that Oswald made purchases at his store were Oswald and Ruby ever in the store at the same time, and to his knowledge Ruby and Oswald were not acquainted....

Dobb's House
Formerly at 1121 North Beckley

Dobbs House was a restaurant in the Oak Cliff neighborhood of Dallas.

Warren Commission testimony of Douglas Leake...

Mr. Douglas Leake... is presently on a shift from 6:00 PM to 6:00 AM [at Dobbs House]. He said that he recalled Jack Ruby as a customer in this restaurant but that Ruby to the best of his recollection had not been seen by him in the restaurant for a year or more prior to November 22, 1963...

Leake stated he never knew of Lee Harvey Oswald by name until Oswald received publicity as a result of the assassination of President Kennedy. He said he then recognized Oswald as having been a customer in the Dobbs House about two times in days prior to the incident. He stated to the best of his recollection Oswald came into the restaurant alone. He advised that he new of no association between Oswald and Ruby and that he never had seen the two of them together.

Ruby apartment
223 South Ewing Apt 207

Jack Ruby moved into apartment 207 at 223 South Ewing in November 1962. He was still living there when the President was assassinated. 223 South Ewing was built in 1962, so it was brand new when Ruby moved in. 223 South Ewing is in the Oak Cliff neighborhood of Dallas, the same neighborhood in which Oswald lived. The apartment building is still there. Its now called the City Inn and Suites. Picture below.

George Senator was Jack Ruby's roommate at 223 South Ewing when Ruby shot Oswald. Senator had previously lived with Ruby at his Marsalis address. In August 1963 Ruby invited Senator to move into his apartment because Senator was having trouble making his rent. (Senator's apartment was next door to Ruby's at 223 S Ewing.)

Testimony of George Senator before the Warren Commission...

Mr. HUBERT. Until January or February of 1962 when you moved in with Jack Ruby; is that correct?

Mr. SENATOR. Yes.

Mr. HUBERT. Where was Ruby living then?

Mr. SENATOR. Ruby was living at the Marsalla----

.....

Mr. HUBERT. How long did you live with Jack then?

Mr. SENATOR. At that time I stayed, I lived with him approximately 5 to 6 months; something like that.

Mr. HUBERT. Anybody else live there with you?

Mr. SENATOR. No; Just Jack and myself.

Mr. HUBERT. What was the occasion for your leaving him?

.....

Mr. SENATOR. Jack likes to live alone in the overall picture. First of all, it is an interference of the time that I wake up and the time that he goes to bed which don't coincide. That is part. And then Jack don't live too clean. I mean he is a type--in other words, he comes home, he is reading a newspaper, on the floor, if he is in the bathroom the newspaper goes on the floor and things of that nature. Though he was very clean about himself, he wasn't clean around the apartment.

.....

[After leaving Ruby's place, Senator moved in with a man named Corbat]

Mr. HUBERT. And how long did you stay with Corbat?

Mr. SENATOR. When I went in with Corbat, of course, he only had a one-bedroom apartment and I had to sleep on the couch again. I slept on so many couches lately. So I told Stan, I told this friend of mine, Corbat, when we were staying on Maple Avenue, that just as soon as I get a little extra money I want to get a two-bedroom apartment and that is where I moved into this last apartment, 225 South Ewing [actually 223 S Ewing].

Mr. HUBERT. That was about when?

Mr. SENATOR. I moved in there, I believe it was the latter part of November of 1962, we found a nice two-bedroom apartment that was very reasonable. I told Jack about it and Jack moved next door.

.....

Mr. SENATOR. Yes; now, the reason Corbat moved out----

Mr. HUBERT. Ruby had another apartment in the same building?

Mr. SENATOR. Yes, yes; we lived, you know, one apartment next to the other. Now, the reason Corbat moved was because he got married August 8, and there I was in the apartment alone and I couldn't handle it alone. But I did stay there 2 months with a struggle.

Mr. HUBERT. So then when did you move from that apartment to Ruby's apartment?

Mr. SENATOR. It was the first week in November of 1963.

.....

Mr. HUBERT. But with reference to the last time you lived with Ruby; that is to say, commencing the beginning of November of 1963?

Mr. SENATOR. Yes.

Mr. HUBERT. You were----

Mr. SENATOR. I was under pressure those 2 months because the rent--you know, when you switch from $62.50 to $125 you are going broke.

Mr. HUBERT. From the time you left Corbat until you moved with Ruby----

Mr. SENATOR. I struggled for the 2 months, and Jack Ruby said to move in, so I moved in.

Mr. HUBERT. And were you supposed to pay any part?

Mr. SENATOR. With Jack, no.

Mr. HUBERT. The arrangement was that you were not to pay anything?

Mr. SENATOR. I wasn't to pay, but you know I would help him. I would help him Fridays and Saturdays, or once in a while I would pop up during a week night.

.....

[Mr. Hubert asks Senator how Ruby reacted to the death of the President.]

Mr. SENATOR. ...I know he was deeply hurt about the President, terribly.

Mr. HUBERT. You say you know that. How do you know that?

Mr. SENATOR. What? By his feelings; by the way he talked about the family and the children; by tears in his eyes, which I have seen, and I am not the only one who has seen it.

Mr. HUBERT. Do you think that he was more disturbed than the average person that you know was disturbed about the President's death?

Mr. SENATOR. All I know, while I can't say about the average because all I know, he was really deeply disturbed, but I can't describe an average because there might be another individual of his nature, too, who knows. Who knows the affections of each and every individual?

.....

[Mr. Hubert asks Senator about the Sunday when Ruby shot Oswald]

Mr. HUBERT. Was Ruby there [in the apartment] when you woke up, or not?

Mr. SENATOR. Yes; he was sleeping.

Mr. HUBERT. When did he waken?

Mr. SENATOR. Ruby must have woke up I assume it probably would have been maybe--of course, I have to guess again--I would assume somewheres around between 9 and 9:30.

127

Mr. HUBERT. Why don't we put it in terms of how much after you did Ruby wake up. In other words, no matter what time you awoke, can you tell us how long after he awakened?

Mr. SENATOR. It could be maybe three-quarters of an hour or an hour. I am not sure.

Mr. HUBERT. What is your first distinct recollection of him that morning?

Mr. SENATOR. Well, the moment he got up he went to the bathroom, which is normal for him.

Mr. HUBERT. Did you speak to him then?

Mr. SENATOR. Yes; I did. Of course, we turned on the TV. He had the TV going. He turned it on to see what the latest news was. Then he went to the bathroom. Of course, then he washed, and he went in and made his own breakfast. I only had coffee. He made himself a couple of scrambled eggs and coffee for himself, and he still had this look which didn't look good.

Mr. HUBERT. Again I want to ask you, can you give us a comparison between the look that he had that morning, which you just described, as opposed to what it was on other occasions in the sense of whether it was growing worse or not?

Mr. SENATOR. He looked a little worse this day here. But if you ask me how to break it down, how he looks worse, how can I express it? The look in his eyes?

Mr. HUBERT. Well, is that one of the things?

Mr. SENATOR. Yes; that is the way it seems.

Mr. HUBERT. The way he talked or what he said?

Mr. SENATOR. The way he talked. He was even mumbling, which I didn't understand. And right after breakfast he got dressed. Then after he got dressed he was pacing the floor from the living room to the bedroom, from the bedroom to the living room, and his lips were going. What he was jabbering I don't know. But he was really pacing. What he was thinking about---

128

Mr. HUBERT. That was after he was dressed?

Mr. SENATOR. Yes; now, what he was thinking about, I don't know what he was thinking about. But he did, which I forgot to tell you, he did get that call from this Little Lynn from Western Union.

Mr. HUBERT. You remember the call?

Mr. SENATOR. Yes.

Mr. HUBERT. Did you answer the phone?

Mr. SENATOR. No; he had already been up.

Mr. HUBERT. How did you know it was Little Lynn?

Mr. SENATOR. I could hear him say. I heard him say Lynn, Western Union. I heard him mention Western Union. I heard about the money and that he was sending it to Fort Worth. She needed $25 for rent.

Mr. HUBERT. Did he tell you that?

Mr. SENATOR. I heard him mention $25 over the phone.

Mr. HUBERT. How did he mention it, that he would send $25?

Mr. SENATOR. He would send $25 to her by Western Union.

Mr. HUBERT. Did he mention that it was for rent?

Mr. SENATOR. Yes; he told me after it was for rent.

Mr. HUBERT. He told you?

Mr. SENATOR. Yes.

.....

Mr. HUBERT. But in any event, he certainly dressed after he got the call, is that correct?

Mr. SENATOR. And after breakfast.

Mr. HUBERT. And after breakfast?

Mr. SENATOR Yes.

Mr. HUBERT. Then after he dressed he paced about some?

Mr. SENATOR Yes.

.....

Mr. HUBERT. All right. Was it at that point that he left?

Mr. SENATOR. Yes.

129

Mr. HUBERT. Did he say anything upon leaving?

Mr. SENATOR. Yes.

Mr. HUBERT. What did he say?

Mr. SENATOR. He said, "George, I am taking the dog down to the club."

Mr. HUBERT. Anything else?

Mr. SENATOR. That was it, and out he went.

.....

Mr. HUBERT. Did he say, when he was coming back?

Mr. SENATOR. No; that is the only words he said when he walked out.

The Tour

1. Start at the Ruth Paine House Museum located at **2515 West Fifth Street in Irving**. Oswald's wife and children were staying here and this is where he picked up the rifle used in the assassination.

Downtown sites

2. Go to the Post Office at **400 N Ervay Street**. This is where Oswald picked up the rifle used to shoot President Kennedy. He had mail ordered it from Klein Sporting Goods in Chicago. (It takes 25 minutes without traffic from the Ruth Paine Museum.)
   - From 2515 West Fifth Street in Irving, head east on W 5th St toward Westbrook Dr (.7 miles)
   - Continue onto W 6th St (.4 miles)
   - Turn right onto S MacArthur Blvd (3.3 miles)
   - Turn left onto I-30 Frontage Rd (.9 miles)
   - Take the Interstate 30 ramp
   - Merge onto I-30 E (7.4 miles)
   - Take exit 45A on the left toward Commerce St/Downtown (.5 miles)
   - Take Commerce St to S Ervay St (1.1 miles)
   - Turn left onto S Ervay St. Destination is on right.

3. Go to the Dallas Municipal Building at **106 N Harwood**. This is where Oswald was jailed after being apprehended at the Texas Theater and where Ruby shot Oswald. Look for the entrance to the underground garage.
   - From 400 N Ervay Street, head northwest on N Ervay St toward Federal St (a little over 100 ft)
   - Turn right at the 1st cross street onto Federal St (300 ft)
   - Turn right onto North St. Paul Street (.2 miles)
   - Slight left onto Pacific Ave (.1 miles)
   - Turn right at the 1st cross street onto N Harwood St
   - Destination will be on the left

4. Go to the Adolphus Hotel at **1321 Commerce Street**. The hotel was across the street from the Carousel Club and Ruby used to hang out there.
   - From 106 N Harwood, head north on N Harwood St toward Elm St (about 250 feet)
   - Turn left at the 1st cross street onto Elm St (.4 miles)
   - Turn left onto N Field St (.1 miles)
   - Turn left at the 2nd cross street onto Commerce St
   - Destination will be on the left

5. Go to the site of the old Carousel Club, Jack Ruby's strip club when JFK was killed. The old location was **1312 ½ Commerce Street**. This is close to S Field Street and Commerce.
   - From 1321 Commerce, walk toward S Field Street.
   - The old site of the Carousel was almost to the corner of Commerce and S Field.

6. Go to the Sante Fe Building at **1114 Commerce Street**. This is where Oswald dropped off his note to FBI agent James Hosty.
   - 1114 Commerce is the next block down from 1312 1/2 Commerce.
   - On Commerce, walk toward Griffin Street. (You cannot drive that way on Commerce. It is one way in the other direction.)

7. Go to the JFK Memorial at **646 Main Street**.
   - The following are directions from the Adolphus Hotel at 1321 Commerce Street.
   - Head east on Commerce St toward S Akard St (150 feet)
   - Turn left onto S Akard St (300 feet)
   - Turn left at the 1st cross street onto Main St (4 ½ blocks)
   - The destination will be on the left

8. Go to the Dallas County Administration Building (formerly the Texas School Book Depository) at **411 Elm Street**. This is where Oswald worked and where he fired the shots killing President Kennedy. The building currently houses the 6th Floor Museum where the sniper's nest has been recreated. You can see the spot where Oswald fired the shots.
   - From 646 Main St, head east on Main St toward Market St
   - Turn left at the 1st cross street onto N Market St
   - Turn left onto Elm St (2 blocks)
   - The destination will be on the right

9. Go to the **grassy knoll.** The grassy knoll is down the hill from the Dallas County Administration Building and towards the triple underpass.

10. **Dealey Plaza**. Walk around Dealey Plaza and see the various plaques.

Oswald's escape route

NOTE: These directions were also presented earlier in the book. It is best to walk Steps 1 – 5, if you are able, and then drive the rest of the way.

1. Start at the Texas Book Depository (now called the Dallas County Administration Building).

2. Walk toward downtown on Elm Street. (NOTE: Commerce is one way, so you cannot drive Elm in this direction.) Go to the entrance to the Renaissance Tower office building located at 1234 Elm – 5 ½ blocks from the Depository. This is approximately where Oswald boarded the bus.

3. Now go back the way you came. This is the way the bus was moving (back toward the scene of the crime). Go to three-quarters of the way between Griffin and Lamar Streets - about 1¼ blocks. This is at 911 Elm Street (Milliners Supply company is located there as of April 2015). Oswald got off the bus here when it became snarled in traffic.

4. Continue to Lamar Street – ¼ block. Turn left.

5. Go on Lamar to the bus station located at **205 Lamar** – 2 blocks. This is where Oswald got the taxi to his rooming house.

   Now you need to get your car and drive the rest of the way.

6. From the Bus Station, drive toward Jackson Street (less than 1 block if you are in front of the bus station).

7. Take a right on Jackson Street.

8. Continue on Jackson Street for three blocks to S Houston.

9. Take a left on S Houston.

10. Continue on S Houston for approximately 2 miles. This will take you to the Houston Street Viaduct that crosses over the Trinity River and into the Oak Cliff neighborhood. NOTE: S Houston turns into Zang Boulevard shortly after you cross the river. Follow Zang to North Beckley.

11. Turn left on North Beckley Avenue.

12. On North Beckley go to Neely Street. This is where Oswald got out of the cab. It is several blocks beyond Oswald's rooming house. He apparently did not want the cab driver to know where he lived.

13. Turn around and drive back the way you came on North Beckley to **1026 North Beckley**. Oswald walked to his rooming house at this address. He went inside, changed clothes and got his handgun.

14. Oswald has exited the rooming house and is walking. Turn around again and proceed on North Beckley toward Neely. Go past Neely one block to E Davis Street.

15. Take a left on E Davis Street.

16. Go ½ block to N Crawford Street and take a right.

17. On N Crawford, go past 7th, 8th and 9th Streets. Proceed into the next block and stop about halfway between 9th Street and Jefferson Boulevard. At this point, Oswald took a left on E 10th Street. E 10th Street, however, no longer exists here due to improvements to WH Adamson High School. You have to take a detour.

18. DETOUR FROM OSWALD'S ROUTE: Go back to E 9th Street. Take a right on 9th Street. Go 1 block to N Patton Avenue. Take a right. Go to E 10th Street.

19. At **E 10th Street and N Patton Avenue**, you are back on Oswald's route. This is close to where Oswald shot Tippit. An historical marker marks the site.

20. On N Patton, go one block to E Jefferson Boulevard. Take a right on E Jefferson.

21. Shortly after going to E Jefferson, Oswald takes off his jacket and throws it in a used car lot. He then proceeds down Jefferson to the Texas Theater. This is almost 6 blocks from N Patton.

22. Go to the Texas Theater at **231 W Jefferson Boulevard**. Oswald hid in the theater and was apprehended there by the Dallas police.

Oak Cliff sites

1. You have already seen a couple of sites in the Oak Cliff neighborhood. Here are some more.

2. From the Texas Theater at 231 W Jefferson Boulevard, go to **223 S Ewing**. This is where Ruby was living when the assassination occurred.
   - From the Texas Theater, head back the way you came on W Jefferson Boulevard - back toward the Tippit killing site (.9 miles)
   - Take a Sharp right onto N Ewing Ave (.2 miles)
   - The destination will be on your right

3. Go to **604 Elsbeth**. This is one of the places Oswald lived.
   - From 223 S Ewing, head north on Ewing Ave toward E 11th St (.2 miles)
   - Right on E Jefferson Blvd (.2 miles)
   - Left onto E 8th St (.5 miles)
   - Continue onto E Davis St (.3 miles)
   - Turn right onto Elsbeth St
   - The destination will be on the right

4. Go to **214 Neely**. This is another place Oswald lived.
   - From 604 Elsbeth, Head north on Elsbeth St toward W Neely St (400 feet)
   - Turn left at the 1st cross street onto W Neely St

5. Go to **500 North Marsalis**. Ruby lived here before he moved to 223 S Ewing.
   - From 214 Neely, head east on W Neely St toward Elsbeth St (.1 miles)
   - Turn right onto N Zang Blvd (500 feet)
   - Turn left onto W Davis St (.2 miles)
   - Continue onto E 8th St (.3 miles)
   - Turn left onto N Marsalis Ave (.2 miles)
   - The destination will be on the right

6. Go to **621 N Marsalis**. Oswald lived here for about a week and then his landlady kicked him out. (It is now a vacant lot).
   - From 500 North Marsalis, head north on N Marsalis Ave toward E 5th St (.1 miles)
   - The destination will be on the left

Other sites

1. Go to **1719 Ervay Street**. Ruby lived in an apartment here in 1952.
   - From 621 N Marsalis, head north on N Marsalis Ave toward Sabine St
   - Continue on E Colorado Blvd. Take E R L Thornton Fwy to Hickory St (2.5 miles)
   - Turn right at the 3rd cross street onto E Colorado Blvd (.4 miles)
   - Turn left onto the ramp to E R L Thornton Fwy (.5 miles)
   - Keep left to continue toward E R L Thornton Fwy (.4 miles)
   - Keep right to continue on Exit 45B, follow signs for Downtown/Griffin St (300 feet)
   - Continue onto E R L Thornton Fwy (.7 miles)
   - Continue onto E R L Thornton Ac Rd S (.2 miles)
   - Turn right onto S Harwood St (.2 miles)
   - Continue on Hickory St. Drive to S Ervay St (.3 miles)
   - Turn right onto Hickory St (.3 miles)
   - Turn right at the 2nd cross street onto S Ervay St
   - The destination will be on the left (400 feet)

2. Go to the location of the old Bob Wills Ranch House (now the Longhorn Ballroom) at **216 Corinth Street**. Ruby owned this club with a partner but lost it due to financial difficulties.
   - From 1719 Ervay Street, Head southeast on S Ervay St toward Beaumont St (.2 miles)
   - Turn right onto Corinth St (.8 miles)
   - The destination will be on your left

3. Go to Parkland Hospital at **5201 Harry Hines Boulevard**.
   - From 216 Corinth St, head south on Corinth St toward S Riverfront Blvd (40 feet)
   - Turn right onto S Riverfront Blvd (1.7 miles)
   - Turn right onto Commerce St/Commerce St Viaduct (.1 miles)
   - Merge onto I-35E N via the ramp to Denton (.2 miles)
   - Merge onto I-35E N (3.2 miles)
   - Take exit 432A toward Inwood Rd (.1 miles)
   - Merge onto N Stemmons Fwy (.3 miles)
   - Turn right onto Inwood Rd (.4 miles)
   - Take the ramp onto Harry Hines Blvd (.5 miles)
   - The destination will be on the right

4. Go to General Edwin Walker's old house at **4011 Turtle Creek Boulevard**. Oswald shot at Walker from the alley behind the house.
   - From 5201 Harry Hines Boulevard, go to Wycliff Avenue (.7 miles)
   - Turn left onto Wycliff Ave (.8 miles)
   - Wycliff Ave turns slightly right and becomes Wycliff-Douglas Connection (.1 miles)
   - Continue onto Douglas Ave (.5 miles)
   - Slight right onto Avondale Ave (.5 miles)
   - Turn left onto Turtle Creek Blvd
   - The destination will be on the left (250 feet)

5. Go to Campisi's Egyptian Restaurant at **5601 E Mockingbird Lane**. Jack Ruby ate here the night before he killed Oswald.
   - From 4011 Turtle Creek Boulevard, head southeast on Turtle Creek Blvd (200 feet)
   - Turn left onto Avondale Ave (.1 miles)
   - Slight right to stay on Avondale Ave (300 feet)
   - Continue onto N Fitzhugh Ave (.5 miles)
   - Turn left onto N Central Expy (1.6 miles)
   - Turn right onto E Mockingbird Ln (.4 miles)
   - Make a U-turn
   - The destination will be on your right

www.ingramcontent.com/pod-product-compliance
Lightning Source LLC
Chambersburg PA
CBHW061147040426
42445CB00013B/1588